life APPLICATION®
STUDY BIBLE
Gospel of John

Life Application Editorial Team:
BRUCE B. BARTON
RONALD A. BEERS
JAMES C. GALVIN
LINDA CHAFFEE TAYLOR
DAVID R. VEERMAN

General Editor:
BRUCE B. BARTON

"How You Can Know God"
(adapted from the *New Believer's Bible*):
GREG LAURIE

NEW LIVING TRANSLATION™

Tyndale House Publishers, Inc.
WHEATON, ILLINOIS

Tyndale House Publishers gratefully acknowledges the role of Youth for Christ/USA in preparing the Life Application Notes and Bible Helps.

Each sale of the New Living Translation benefits Wycliffe Bible Translators, which completed its four hundredth New Testament in 1995 and is currently working in another 1,000 languages. Tyndale House Publishers and Wycliffe Bible Translators share the vision for an understandable, accurate translation of the Bible for every person.

With 40 million copies in print, *The Living Bible* has been meeting a great need in people's hearts for more than thirty years. But even good things can be improved, so ninety evangelical scholars from various theological backgrounds and denominations were commissioned in 1989 to begin revising *The Living Bible*. The end result of this seven-year process is the *Holy Bible,* New Living Translation—a general-purpose translation that is accurate, easy to read, and excellent for study.

The goal of any Bible translation is to convey the meaning of the ancient Hebrew and Greek texts as accurately as possible to the modern reader. The New Living Translation is based on the most recent scholarship in the theory of translation. The challenge for the translators was to create a text that would make the same impact in the life of modern readers that the original text had for the original readers. In the New Living Translation, this is accomplished by translating entire thoughts (rather than just words) into natural, everyday English. The end result is a translation that is easy to read and understand and that accurately communicates the meaning of the original text.

We believe that this new translation, which combines the latest in scholarship with the best in translation style, will speak to your heart. We present the New Living Translation with the prayer that God will use it to speak his timeless truth to the church and to the world in a fresh, new way. The complete Bible will be available in the New Living Translation text in August 1996.

The Publishers
January 1996

TRANSLATION TEAM

PENTATEUCH

Daniel I. Block, General Reviewer
The Southern Baptist Theological Seminary

GENESIS
Allan Ross, *Trinity Episcopal Seminary*
John Sailhamer, *Northwestern College*
Gordon Wenham, *The Cheltenham and Gloucester College of Higher Education*

EXODUS
Robert Bergen, *Hannibal-LaGrange College*
Daniel I. Block, *The Southern Baptist Theological Seminary*
Eugene Carpenter, *Bethel College, Mishawaka, Indiana*

LEVITICUS
David Baker, *Ashland Theological Seminary*
Victor Hamilton, *Asbury College*
Kenneth Mathews, *Beeson Divinity School, Samford University*

NUMBERS
Dale A. Brueggemann, *Assemblies of God, Division of Foreign Missions*
Roland K. Harrison (deceased), *Wycliffe College*
Gerald L. Mattingly, *Johnson Bible College*

DEUTERONOMY
J. Gordon McConville, *The Cheltenham and Gloucester College of Higher Education*
Eugene H. Merrill, *Dallas Theological Seminary*
John A. Thompson, *University of Melbourne*

HISTORICAL BOOKS

Barry J. Beitzel, General Reviewer
Trinity Evangelical Divinity School

JOSHUA/ JUDGES
Carl E. Armerding, *Schloss Mittersill Study Centre*
Barry J. Beitzel, *Trinity Evangelical Divinity School*
Lawson Stone, *Asbury Theological Seminary*

1 & 2 SAMUEL
Barry J. Beitzel, *Trinity Evangelical Divinity School*
V. Philips Long, *Covenant Theological Seminary*
J. Robert Vannoy, *Biblical Theological Seminary*

1 & 2 KINGS
Bill T. Arnold, *Asbury Theological Seminary*
William H. Barnes, *Southeastern College of the Assemblies of God*
Frederic W. Bush, *Fuller Theological Seminary*

1 & 2 CHRONICLES
Raymond B. Dillard (deceased), *Westminster Theological Seminary*
David A. Dorsey, *Evangelical School of Theology*
Terry Eves, *Calvin College*

EZRA/ NEHEMIAH/ ESTHER/ RUTH
William C. Williams, *Southern California College*
Hugh G. M. Williamson, *Oxford University*

POETRY

Tremper Longman III, General Reviewer
Westminster Theological Seminary

JOB
August Konkel, *Providence Theological Seminary*
Tremper Longman III, *Westminster Theological Seminary*
Al Wolters, *Redeemer College*

PSALMS 1–75
Mark D. Futato, *Westminster Theological Seminary in California*
Douglas Green, *Westminster Theological Seminary*
Richard Pratt, *Reformed Theological Seminary*

PSALMS 76–150
David M. Howard Jr., *Trinity Evangelical Divinity School*
Raymond C. Ortlund Jr., *Trinity Evangelical Divinity School*
Willem VanGemeren, *Trinity Evangelical Divinity School*

PROVERBS
Ted Hildebrandt, *Grace College*
Richard Schultz, *Wheaton College*
Raymond C. Van Leeuwen, *Eastern College*

ECCLESIASTES/ SONG OF SONGS
Daniel C. Fredericks, *Belhaven College*
David Hubbard, *Fuller Theological Seminary*
Tremper Longman III, *Westminster Theological Seminary*

PROPHETS

John N. Oswalt, General Reviewer
Asbury Theological Seminary

ISAIAH
John N. Oswalt, *Asbury Theological Seminary*
Gary Smith, *Bethel Theological Seminary*
John Walton, *Moody Bible Institute*

JEREMIAH/ LAMENTATIONS
G. Herbert Livingston, *Asbury Theological Seminary*
Elmer A. Martens, *Mennonite Brethren Biblical Seminary*

EZEKIEL
Daniel I. Block, *The Southern Baptist Theological Seminary*
David H. Engelhard, *Calvin Theological Seminary*
David Thompson, *Asbury Theological Seminary*

DANIEL/ HAGGAI/ ZECHARIAH/ MALACHI
Joyce Baldwin Caine (deceased), *Trinity College, Bristol*
Douglas Gropp, *Catholic University of America*
Roy Hayden, *Oral Roberts School of Theology*

HOSEA–ZEPHANIAH
Joseph Coleson, *Nazarene Theological Seminary*
Andrew Hill, *Wheaton College*
Richard Patterson, *Professor Emeritus, Liberty University*

GOSPELS AND ACTS

Grant R. Osborne, General Reviewer
Trinity Evangelical Divinity School

MATTHEW
Craig Blomberg, *Denver Conservative Baptist Seminary*
Donald A. Hagner, *Fuller Theological Seminary*
David Turner, *Grand Rapids Baptist Seminary*

MARK
Robert Guelich (deceased), *Fuller Theological Seminary*
Grant R. Osborne, *Trinity Evangelical Divinity School*

LUKE
Darrel Bock, *Dallas Theological Seminary*
Scot McKnight, *North Park College*
Robert Stein, *Bethel Theological Seminary*

JOHN
Gary M. Burge, *Wheaton College*
Philip W. Comfort, *Wheaton College*
Marianne Meye Thompson, *Fuller Theological Seminary*

ACTS
D. A. Carson, *Trinity Evangelical Divinity School*
William J. Larkin, *Columbia Biblical Seminary*
Roger Mohrlang, *Whitworth College*

LETTERS AND REVELATION

Norman R. Ericson, General Reviewer
Wheaton College

ROMANS/ GALATIANS
Gerald Borchert, *The Southern Baptist Theological Seminary*
Douglas J. Moo, *Trinity Evangelical Divinity School*
Thomas R. Schreiner, *Bethel Theological Seminary*

1 & 2 CORINTHIANS
Joseph Alexanian, *Trinity International University*
Linda Belleville, *North Park Theological Seminary*
Douglas A. Oss, *Central Bible College*
Robert Sloan, *Baylor University*

EPHESIANS–PHILEMON
Harold W. Hoehner, *Dallas Theological Seminary*
Moises Silva, *Gordon-Conwell Theological Seminary*
Klyne Snodgrass, *North Park Theological Seminary*

HEBREWS/ JAMES/ 1 & 2 PETER/ JUDE
Peter Davids, *Canadian Theological Seminary*
Norman R. Ericson, *Wheaton College*
William Lane, *Seattle Pacific University*
J. Ramsey Michaels, *S. W. Missouri State University*

1–3 JOHN/ REVELATION
Greg Beale, *Gordon-Conwell Theological Seminary*
Robert Mounce, *Whitworth College*
M. Robert Mulholland, *Asbury Theological Seminary*

SPECIAL REVIEWERS

F. F. Bruce (deceased), *University of Manchester*
Kenneth N. Taylor, *Tyndale House Publishers*

COORDINATING TEAM

Mark R. Norton, Managing Editor and O.T. Coordinating Editor
Philip W. Comfort, N.T. Coordinating Editor
Ronald A. Beers, Executive Director and Stylist
Mark D. Taylor, Director and Chief Stylist

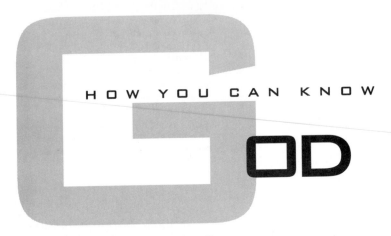

What Is Missing in Our Lives?

Purpose, meaning, a reason for living—these are all things we desire and search for in life. Despite steps each one of us takes to find purpose and meaning in life, we still feel empty, unfulfilled. That is because there is a spiritual emptiness in each of our lives. We each have a hole in our heart, a spiritual vacuum deep within our soul—a "God-shaped blank." Possessions won't fill this hole, nor will success. Relationships alone cannot satisfy this emptiness, and morality, in and of itself, falls miserably short of occupying this space. In fact, even religion cannot fill the void in our heart (see John 4:13-15; 5:39-40; 6:63-65).

There is only one way to effectively fill that void. This way will not only help us to have a life that is full and rich on this earth, but—more importantly—give us the absolute hope of spending eternity in the presence of God. Before we can truly appreciate this good news though, we need to understand the bad news, which is a serious problem we all have.

THE PROBLEM: SIN

The Bible clearly identifies our serious problem as sin. Sin is not just an act but the actual nature of our being. In other words, we are not sinners because we sin. Rather, we sin because we are sinners! We are born with a nature to do wrong. King David, the Old Testament Israelite ruler, wrote, "For I was born a sinner—yes, from the moment my mother conceived me" (Psalm 51:5). Because we are born sinners, sinning comes to all of us naturally. That is why it is futile to think that the answer to all of life's problems comes from "within." According to the Bible, the *problem* is within! Scripture tells us, "The human heart is most deceitful and desperately wicked. Who really knows how bad it is?" (Jeremiah 17:9).

We are not basically good—we are basically sinful. This sinfulness spills out into everything we do. Every problem we experience in our society today can be traced back to our refusal to live God's way. Clear back to the Garden of Eden, Adam made his choice, and he suffered the consequences of it, setting the pattern that all humanity would follow. The Bible explains, "When Adam sinned, sin entered the entire human race. Adam's sin brought death, so death spread to everyone, for everyone sinned. . . . Yes, Adam's one sin brought condemnation upon everyone" (Romans 5:12, 18).

"That's not fair!" you may protest. Why should we suffer because of what someone else has done? Yet, given the opportunity, each one of us would have done the same thing as Adam. In fact, not a single day passes that we do not face the same test that was set before Adam. God has given us the freedom to choose between two separate paths: the path that leads to life and the path that leads to death. The Bible says, "Today I have given you the choice between life and death, between blessings and curses. I call on heaven and earth to witness the choice you make. Oh, that you would choose life, that you and your descendants might live!" (Deuteronomy 30:19).

 # The Solution: Jesus Christ

God understood our problem and knew that we could do nothing about it. Because God loves us, he sent his own Son, Jesus Christ, to earth to bridge the chasm of sin that separates us from him (see John 3:1-16; 6:47; 8:24).

WHY JESUS CAN BRIDGE THE GAP

There has never been anyone like Jesus. For starters, Jesus was not conceived in the womb of his mother through natural means. Rather, he was supernaturally conceived in the womb of a young virgin named Mary. Because of his supernatural conception, Jesus, who is wholly God, also became wholly human.

Though Jesus is God, he chose to lay aside the privileges of his deity to live on earth as a man. The Bible, describing the sacrifice Christ made in becoming a man, says that Jesus "made himself nothing; he took the humble position of a slave and appeared in human form. And in human form he obediently humbled himself even further by dying a criminal's death on a cross" (Philippians 2:7-8). It is extremely important to note that Jesus did not cease to be God when he came to earth. He simply laid aside his divine privileges and walked the earth as a man. In doing so, he was personally able to experience the gamut of human emotions, ranging from happiness to deep sorrow. He felt what it was like to be tired, cold, and hungry.

Moreover, he came to this earth with a clear objective in mind: to bridge that gap between us and God.

When the Israelites of the Old Testament sinned, they would have the high priest go into the Temple and offer an animal sacrifice to God to atone for their sins. In a symbolic sense, this was a way of putting one's sins on the animal, which stood in the place of the guilty person. The Bible teaches, "Without the shedding of blood, there is no forgiveness of sins" (Hebrews 9:22).

The sacrificial rituals carried out by the Israelites in the Old Testament foreshadowed what Jesus would do when he came to this earth. He took the sin of the world upon himself when he hung on the cross so many years ago.

Numerous Old Testament prophecies pointed not only to his birth and life, but also to his death, including the way in which he would die.

Jesus knew from the beginning that he had come expressly to die for the sins of humanity. He also knew that this sacrifice would be made on a Roman cross. He began his final journey to the cross of Calvary at a place called Caesarea Philippi, and he often spoke of his impending death with his disciples. Scripture records, "From then on Jesus began to tell his disciples plainly that he had to go to Jerusalem, and he told them what would happen to him there. He would suffer at the hands of the leaders and the leading priests and the teachers of religious law. He would be killed, and he would be raised on the third day" (Matthew 16:21).

He was eventually arrested on false charges after Judas Iscariot, one of his own disciples, betrayed him. But it was no accident. If humanity was going to be put in touch with God and have the barrier that separated them removed, something drastic had to be done. In essence, with one hand Jesus took hold of a Holy God, and with the other hand he took hold of the sinful human race. As crude nails were pounded into his hands, he bridged the gap for us!

We must not forget, however, that three days after his crucifixion, Jesus rose from the dead! If it is true that "you can't keep a good man down," then it is even truer that you can't keep the "God-man" down.

The Response: Accept God's Offer

To know Jesus Christ personally and have your sin forgiven, you must believe that you are a sinner separated from God and that your only hope is Jesus Christ, the Son of God, who came and died for your sins. To stop here, however, would be to stop short of salvation.

There are two things you must now do to enter into a relationship with the God from whom you have been separated.

1. TURN FROM YOUR SINS

As Jesus began his public ministry, his first message was, "Turn from your sins" (Mark 1:15). He was telling the people to repent—to acknowledge their sins, change their minds, and change the direction of their lives.

Look at it this way. In the past, we have been blinded by our sin, causing us to run from God. As we repent, we do a "U-turn" and start running toward him. It is not enough just to be sorry for our sins. We must also change our lifestyle, for the Bible teaches that "God can use sorrow in our lives to help us turn away from sin and seek salvation" (2 Corinthians 7:10). In other words, if you are really sorry for something, it will result in a change in your actions.

The apostle Paul summed up this change succinctly when he quoted Jesus, who said that people must "turn from the darkness to light, and from the power of Satan to God. Then they will receive forgiveness for their sins and be given a place among God's people, who are set apart by faith in me" (Acts 26:18).

You see, there are some things only God can do and some things only you can do. Only God can remove your sins and give you the gift of eternal life, but only you can turn from your sins and receive Jesus as your Savior. That brings up the second thing you must do to respond to God's offer.

2. BELIEVE IN AND RECEIVE JESUS CHRIST INTO YOUR LIFE

Having seen the enormity of your sin and having decided to turn away from it, you then must believe in and receive Jesus Christ as your Lord and Savior. Becoming a Christian, however, is far more than following a creed or trying to live by certain standards. Jesus said that you must be "born again," or more literally, "born from above" (John 3:3). This spiritual rebirth happens when we personally believe in Jesus Christ, receive him by inviting him into our lives, and turn from our sins. In other words, we ask Jesus to come and take residence in our life, making the changes he deems necessary. A person must take this all-important step in order to become a child of God.

Notice that this offer is yours for the asking, and it is free. You don't have to work for it, trying to clean up your life before you make this life-changing decision. The Bible says, "The free gift of God is eternal life through Christ Jesus our Lord" (Romans 6:23).

Being a Christian also means having a relationship with the living God. In Revelation 3:20, Jesus said, "Look! Here I stand at the door and knock. If you hear me calling and open the door, I will come in, and we will share a meal as friends." To better understand the meaning of this verse, it is important to understand the culture at the time it was written. Eating together in Bible times was a long, drawn-out affair. People would not sit on chairs behind tables in a formal setting as we do, but they would often sit on the ground, reclining on pillows around a low table. The relaxed atmosphere made meals a time when you would not only satisfy your appetite but also receive a gratifying serving of enjoyable table conversation. You would share your heart and life with those who sat beside you.

Consequently, when Jesus says that he will "share a meal" with us, it implies intimacy, closeness, and friendship. He offers this to us, but we must first "hear him calling" us.

To hear God calling us, we must know how he speaks. One way in which God speaks to us is described on occasion as a "still, small voice." This could be described in another way as that tug you may have felt on your heart from the Holy Spirit showing you your need for Jesus. He may even be speaking to you right now! It is at that point that you must "open the door." Only you can do that. Jesus will not force his way in.

RECEIVING JESUS CHRIST INTO YOUR HEART

If you are ready to turn from your sins and believe in Jesus Christ so that you can receive the forgiveness of sin and the hope of eternal life, then take a moment to bow your head and pray a prayer like this one right now:

God, I'm sorry for my sin. I turn from it right now. I thank you for sending Jesus Christ to die on the cross for my sin.

Jesus, I ask you to come into my heart and life right now. Be my Lord, Savior, and friend. Help me to follow you all the days of my life as your disciple.

Thank you for forgiving and receiving me right now. Thank you that my sin is forgiven and that I am going to heaven. In Jesus' name I pray, Amen.

REDEDICATING YOUR LIFE TO JESUS CHRIST

Perhaps you are already a Christian, but you have strayed from Jesus Christ. You have been a prodigal son or daughter. God will forgive you right now if you will return to him. He tells us in Scripture, "My wayward children, come back to me, and I will heal your wayward hearts" (Jeremiah 3:22). If you would like to return to God and rededicate your life to him right now, you may want to pray something like this:

God, I am sorry for my sin. I am sorry that I have strayed from you. I ask you to forgive me now as I repent of my sin. I don't want to live like a prodigal any longer.

Renew and revive me as I once again follow you as my God. Thank you for your forgiveness. In Jesus' name I pray, Amen.

Whether you prayed to make a first time commitment or a recommitment, you have made the right decision. God has forgiven and received you if you really meant it. Know that your relationship with Jesus Christ will bring radical and dramatic changes in your life. Describing this, the Bible says, "Those who become Christians become new persons. They are not the same anymore, for the old life is gone. A new life has begun!" (2 Corinthians 5:17). Now that is good news! But more importantly, God has changed your eternal destiny. Instead of fearing eternal punishment in a place called hell, you will spend peaceful eternity in his presence in heaven.

Who Is Jesus?

Throughout history many people have attempted to answer this question. Some have done so accurately, but many have not. Our best source for answering this question is—once again—God's own Word. The Bible presents us with some inescapable truths about Jesus that demand a response. Anyone who seriously studies Scripture to learn more about Jesus must answer two probing questions: (1) "What do you think of Jesus Christ?" and (2) "Who is he?" The writer C. S. Lewis made this observation: "You must make your choice. Either this man was and is the Son of God or else he is a madman or something worse. You can shut him up for a fool, you can spit at him and kill him as a demon, or you can fall at his feet and call him Lord and God. But let us not come with any patronizing nonsense about his being a great human teacher. He has not left that open to us. He did not intend to" (*Mere Christianity*, bk. II, chapter 3, pp. 55-56).

Jesus was not just a good man. He was—and is—the God-man. Let's examine what the Bible has to say about Jesus.

1. **Jesus Is Human** Jesus became our supreme example as God in human form (see John 3:27-34; Philippians 2:5-11).
2. **Jesus Is Divine** Even though Jesus became human, he still remained God (see John 1:1-14; Colossians 1:15-20).
3. **Jesus Had a Specific Mission to Accomplish** Jesus came to save humankind from sin (see Luke 4:16-21; John 12:23-26).
4. **Jesus Made the Ultimate Sacrifice** Jesus endured tremendous pain so that we could enjoy eternity with him (see Isaiah 52:13–53:12; John 19).
5. **Jesus Has Great Power to Transform People** Jesus can change the most unlikely person into one of the most powerful witnesses on his behalf (see Acts 9:1-19).
6. **Jesus Has an Eternal Dominion** Jesus' Kingdom extends beyond the boundaries of space and time (see John 14:1-7; Revelation 1:4-8).

Who Is the Holy Spirit?

The Holy Spirit is the most mysterious member of the Trinity, which includes God the Father, God the Son (Jesus Christ), and God the Spirit (or the Holy Spirit). Many struggle with the idea of God being three persons, yet one. Quite honestly, we will never fully grasp the concept this side of heaven.

Some, however, have wrongly thought of the Holy Spirit as more of an "it" than a "him." That is probably due in part to biblical descriptions of him as being like the wind or coming upon Jesus in the form of a dove, among other comparisons. Yet these descriptions must be balanced with the descriptions of the other members of the Trinity. For instance, Jesus referred to himself as "the bread of life," and "the good shepherd." In the same way, God the Father is referred to as "a refuge" and "a consuming fire." Does this mean that Jesus is a loaf of bread or a sheep farmer, or that the Father is a pile of rocks or a blast furnace? Of course not! These are simply metaphors used in Scripture to help communicate God's character. Likewise, the unique descriptions attributed to the Holy Spirit do not imply that the Holy Spirit is merely some "force" or "power." Jesus said this about the Holy Spirit: "When the Spirit of truth comes, he will guide you into all truth. . . . He will tell you about the future" (John 16:13). Note the use of the pronoun *he.* The Holy Spirit has a distinct personality, and he also has specific work that he wants to do in our lives as followers of Jesus Christ. Explore what the Bible says about him.

1. **Who the Holy Spirit Helps** The Holy Spirit strengthens and empowers followers of Christ (see John 16:5-7; Acts 2:1-40).
2. **How the Holy Spirit Works with the Father and the Son** The Holy Spirit works alongside God the Father and Jesus, God's Son, to make our lives pleasing to God (see 1 Peter 1:2).
3. **Why God Gives Us the Holy Spirit** The Holy Spirit's presence in our lives is God's mark of ownership (see Ephesians 1:13-14).
4. **How the Holy Spirit Works in Our Lives** The Holy Spirit draws us to Christ, enters our life at conversion, and empowers us as we allow him to work in our life (see John 14:15-17).
5. **Why Christians Need the Holy Spirit** Living the Christian life is impossible without the Holy Spirit's help (see Galatians 5:16-25).

Love

On one occasion Jesus was asked what commandment was the most important. He replied, "The most important commandment is this: 'Hear, O Israel! The Lord our God is the one and only Lord. And you must love the Lord your God with all your heart, all your soul, all your mind, and all your strength.' The second is equally important: 'Love your neighbor as yourself'" (Mark 12:29-31).

If you truly love God with all your heart, soul, mind, and strength, you will want to do what pleases him. In the same way, if you really love others as much as you love yourself, you will be concerned for their welfare and treat them accordingly. Before you can effectively love God, however, you must first realize how much he loves you.

Scripture explains that God showed his great love for us by sending Christ to die for us while we were still sinners who had no relationship with him (Romans 5:8). The more we realize this wonderful truth, the more our love for God will grow. These Scripture passages explore some different facets of the love we should have for God and for others.

1. **God Should Be the Greatest Love of Our Life** Before we can fully love one another, we must fully love God and understand his love for us (see Deuteronomy 6:4-5; 1 John 4:19).
2. **Christ's Love Sets the Standard** Our love for others should model Christ's love for us (see John 15:9-14; Ephesians 5:2).
3. **Love Surpasses All Spiritual Gifts** A Christian who understands what love truly means and shows love in his or her life is the greatest testimony to others (see 1 Corinthians 13).
4. **Our Love for God Prepares Us for Service** The depth of our love for God directly affects our ability to minister to others (see John 21:15-17).
5. **Our Love for Others Mirrors the Condition of Our Heart** The love we have for those around us is an indication of the strength of our Christian walk (see John 13:34-35; 1 John 2:9-11).
6. **Our Love Should Grow** The closer we grow to God, the more our love for others should increase (see 1 Thessalonians 3:12-13).

Forgiveness

One of the great principles of the Christian life is forgiveness. Jesus modeled this principle for us when he hung on the cross and prayed for the very people who had put him there (see Luke 23:34). His words were so powerful and unexpected that they brought about the conversion of one of the thieves hanging on a cross next to him.

Because Jesus completely forgave us, he wants us to follow his example by forgiving others. As Scripture says, "Be kind to each other, tenderhearted, forgiving one another, just as God through Christ has forgiven you. Follow God's example in everything you do, because you are his dear children" (Ephesians 4:32–5:1). The Bible gives us several important characteristics of the forgiveness we should have for others.

1. **Forgiveness First Comes from God** Our forgiveness of others should flow from God's forgiveness of us (see Mark 11:25).
2. **Forgiveness Knows No Limits** For a Christian, no wrong is too great or too small to forgive (see Matthew 18:21-35).
3. **Forgiveness Is Not Selective** You can't choose to forgive some people and not forgive others (see Matthew 5:43-48).
4. **Forgiveness Breaks Down Walls** When you choose to forgive, you experience true freedom (see Genesis 45:1-15).

Faith and Works

When a person truly comes to Jesus Christ, this relationship will dramatically transform his or her life. We may see this transformation more immediately in the lives of some than others. For those whose lives are characterized by pronounced bad habits and blatant immoral living, the change in lifestyle will show others that something profound has indeed happened within that person's life. For others who may not be known for blatantly sinful living, the change may not be as outwardly pronounced, but it is just as significant. Remember, all of us were separated from God by sin, which was dealt with and atoned for at the cross of Jesus.

Our conversion will show itself in both fruit and works. This concept of "bearing fruit" is used often in Scripture to describe the results of someone's commitment to Jesus Christ. If we do not bear fruit, then it is apparent we have not really come to know Jesus Christ as Lord and Savior. Bearing fruit is not an option. It is the natural result of a person coming into union with God. Sometimes there is confusion in this area of fruitbearing, or works. See what the Bible has to say about the issue.

1. **Our Lives Should Show That God Is at Work in Our Hearts** God desires that we demonstrate our spiritual growth through our outward actions (see Romans 7:4).
2. **We Must Live Out Our Faith** Faith without deeds is incomplete (see James 2:14-18).
3. **God Saved Us for a Purpose** While God himself gave us salvation, he planned that our salvation would lead to good works (see Ephesians 2:10).
4. **Our Walk Should Match Our Talk** God isn't as concerned with what we *say* we believe as with how we *live* what we believe (see Matthew 7:21-23).

Peace

Peace of mind—it seems almost elusive in a day when murders are commonplace, job security is nonexistent, and the moral fabric of society is tearing apart at the seams. Yet Jesus has promised that each one of us can experience true peace: "I am leaving you with a gift—peace of mind and heart. And the peace I give isn't like the peace the world gives. So don't be troubled or afraid" (John 14:27).

Unfortunately, some people are so caught up in the "pursuit of peace," that they have forgotten that Jesus has already given it to them. They have simply left that gift "unopened." And we cannot find peace outside of the parameters God has given us. As Augustine said many years ago, "Our souls are restless until they find their rest in God." Begin to "unwrap" this precious gift by examining what God's Word has to say about it.

1. **Peace Begins When We Relinquish Control of Our Lives to God** When we give Jesus our burdens and allow him to guide us, we find rest (see Matthew 11:28-30; John 16:33).
2. **Perfect Peace Builds upon Total Trust** As God becomes a regular part of our daily lives, our worries begin to disappear (see Isaiah 26:3).
3. **Our Peace Continues As We Follow the Holy Spirit** We must stop allowing our old, sinful nature to control us before we can really experience peace (see Romans 8:5-8).
4. **A Love for God's Word Brings Peace of Mind** The more the Bible becomes a part of our lives, the greater the peace we will experience (see Psalm 119:165-168).
5. **God's Peace Needs to Rule in Our Hearts** We must constantly keep other things from crowding out God's peace in our lives (see John 14:27-29; Colossians 3:15).

Purity

Purity is a quality we hear too little about today. Usually when we do hear something about purity, it is in reference to sexual purity. But purity goes beyond this to include wholesome thoughts, a sincere desire to do what is right, and a commitment to obey God's Word. Jesus alluded to the importance of purity by promising that those whose hearts were pure would see God (Matthew 5:8). In using the word *heart,* Jesus was saying that the center of our being—our will, our emotions, and our thought processes—needs to be cleansed of sin. The Bible texts below examine the idea of purity and how it affects us as followers of Jesus Christ.

1. **Don't Place Yourself in the Way of Unnecessary Temptation** Know your moral weaknesses, and avoid situations where the temptation to sin would be irresistible (see James 1:14-15).
2. **Guard the Content of Your Thoughts** Don't fill your mind with the world's moral filth (see 2 Timothy 2:22).
3. **Beware of the Sins of the Heart** The person who commits adultery in his heart is just as guilty as the person who actually carries it out (see Matthew 5:27-30).
4. **Avoid Adulterous Relationships** God specifically warns us against living in immoral relationships (see John 8:1-11; 1 Thessalonians 4:1-8).
5. **If You Fall, Ask God to Forgive You and Purify Your Heart and Desires** Only God can forgive you, restore your joy, and fill you with the right desires (see Psalm 51:7-15).
6. **Keep an Eternal Perspective** Don't waste your time chasing after earthly pleasures (see 2 Peter 3:10-11).
7. **Live to Please God** Surrendering your life to the leading of the Holy Spirit is the only way to live a life that is pleasing to God (see Romans 8:5-8).

Perseverance

There will be times in your Christian walk when you will feel emotionally "down." You may think that God has forgotten about you. Or you might become discouraged as you see others who have professed faith in Jesus Christ lose interest in spiritual things and fall away. You may begin to wonder whether you are next on the Devil's "hit list." But God will not allow you to be hit with more than you can handle spiritually. In fact, it is during times of trouble that you will actually be strengthened, not weakened.

As you read your Bible, you will come across words like *endurance* and *perseverance.* These words are often used when the Bible compares the Christian life to a race. The race referred to is a marathon, not a fifty-yard dash. Because the Christian life is a long-distance run, you need to pace yourself, to persevere, and most of all, to *finish* the race. Look up the following passages that describe how and why you need to persevere through the inevitable struggles of life.

1. **Perseverance Produces Results** As you steadily grow in your understanding of God's Word and apply it to your life, you will win others to the Lord (see Luke 8:15).
2. **Life's Trials Will Make You Stronger** You shouldn't view difficulties as obstacles to your faith, but as opportunities for spiritual growth (see James 1:2-4).
3. **Christ Endured Great Pain for Us** Jesus modeled the ultimate in endurance so that we would be encouraged to keep our faith strong in the race of life (see Hebrews 12:1-3).
4. **God Honors Those Who Persevere** A wholehearted commitment to God will enable you to "finish well" with your faith intact (see Joshua 14:6-14).

Joy

One noticeable change that takes place in a new believer's life is the inner joy he or she receives. In fact, joy is listed as part of the "fruit of the Spirit" that should be evident in a believer's life (see Galatians 5:22). But this joy is different from the fleeting and temporary "happiness" that is usually dependent upon "good things" happening in someone's life. While sorrows will come a believer's way, the Holy Spirit gives him or her an inner joy and peace that cannot be taken away. Below are some of the ways in which you can experience God's joy in your life.

1. **Studying God's Word Helps Us to Experience His Joy** As we study God's Word and honor God with our lives, we experience his joy in our lives (see Nehemiah 8:1-18).
2. **Knowing and Trusting God Is the Source of Inexpressible Joy** The greatest joy we can experience comes only from a personal relationship with Jesus Christ (see 1 Peter 1:8).
3. **Sharing Your Faith Results in Joy** While laboring to introduce people to Jesus is difficult work, the end result will give you much to celebrate (see John 4:34-36).
4. **Overlooking Petty Issues Frees Us to Experience Joy** God wants us to experience his joy in our lives and to avoid those things that could hamper that joy (see 1 Corinthians 1:10-17).
5. **Knowing Who You Belong to and What the Future Holds Brings True Joy** Realizing that you are a child of God and that you will spend eternity in heaven with him will bring you joy (see John 15:9-11; Romans 15:13).

Honesty and Integrity

Honesty and integrity seem to be in short supply these days. Yet the Bible tells us that they are a part of the godly man or woman's life. Unfortunately, the world tends to gloss over that aspect of the Christian life. It wants to characterize Christians as people who are out of touch with reality. But a Christian is simply someone who allows God to influence every aspect of his or her life—down to the practical, everyday dealings of business, finances, and relationships. The following passages examine how honesty and integrity should characterize our lives.

1. **We Should Be above Criticism** Daniel's faithful and honest lifestyle made him "stand apart" from everyone else (see Daniel 6:3-4).
2. **Our Conduct Should Cause Others to Glorify Christ** Living a good, honest life around our unbelieving neighbors will ultimately bring glory to God (see 1 Peter 2:9-12).
3. **We Need to Set an Example for Others** We must seriously pursue a life of integrity in order to be a solid example for our fellow Christians (see Titus 2:6-8).

Marriage

How many times have you heard the cliché "They have a marriage made in heaven"? This statement implies that some marriages are destined to be good, while others are destined to be bad. Such thinking assumes that marriage has a life of its own, and the only way to find out if you are to have a "good" one or a "bad" one is to "give it a shot." What most people don't seem to understand, though, is that marriage is like a mirror. It reflects what it sees. If a marriage is strong, it is because the husband and wife have put a lot of hard work into it. If a marriage is weak, it is because the husband or wife or both have neglected it.

God never intended for anyone to have a weak marriage. His design for marriage is life-long, fulfilling companionship. For a couple's marriage to thrive within his design, the couple must obey God and his Word and lay aside this world's distorted and perverse concept of marriage. The Bible contains truths that will not only help keep a couple together but will also keep their marriage strong. In fact, the lessons this book gives on marriage should serve as the foundation of every Christian couple's relationship. Whether you are married or single, the following verses will give you a godly perspective on marriage relationships.

1. **God Created Marriage** We can learn more about God's marriage ideal from the world's first husband and wife (see Genesis 2:15-25).
2. **Husbands and Wives Have Distinct Roles in Marriage** A marriage works when a couple follows God's specific design for the husband and the wife (see Ephesians 5:21-33).
3. **The Boundaries of Marriage Are to Be Honored and Enjoyed** Sexual intimacy is meant to be enjoyed only within the bounds of the marriage relationship (see Proverbs 5:15-20).
4. **Keeping Your Marriage Strong** God promises punishment to those who commit adultery or lead immoral lives (see Hebrews 13:4).
5. **Divorce Is Not Part of God's Plan** Jesus teaches that marriage is meant to be a lifelong commitment (see Mark 10:2-12).
6. **A Christian Should Not Leave a Non-Christian Spouse** An unbelieving husband or wife should not be abandoned, but loved (see 1 Corinthians 7:12-16).
7. **Marriage Is Not for Everyone** Though God blesses many with marriage, some are given a calling—an ability—to remain single (see 1 Corinthians 7:1-40).
8. **Marriage Is for Companionship** While God has given some the ability to remain happily single, he has given others the gift of a companion for life (see Proverbs 18:22).
9. **There Is an Intimacy in Marriage That Can Be Found Nowhere Else** God wants you to have a fulfilling, enjoyable sex life within the parameters of marriage (see Song of Songs 4:1–5:1).
10. **A Strong Marriage Is an Ideal Environment for Raising Godly Children** Those children who see their parents united by their love for God and one another have a distinct advantage over those who do not (see Malachi 2:15).

 # Parents/Children

God's plan is to build, strengthen, and protect the family. Satan's plan is to undermine, weaken, and destroy it. Make no mistake: Satan has declared war on the family. Tragically, many of us have been willing accomplices. Why? Because the bulk of the problems in our culture today can be directly traced to the breakdown of the family or to homes in which biblical principles are ignored or disobeyed. This not only includes husbands and wives splitting apart, but also "alternative families," such as homosexual marriages and "live-in" lovers. Such relationships will never be blessed or honored by God, for they are clearly outside the parameters of his will. It has been said, "A family can survive without a country, but a country cannot survive without the family."

Fortunately, there is hope. The Bible gives us specific guidelines to follow when it comes to parenting. If they are put into practice, we will see amazing results. See what the Bible has to say about raising children who love and reverence the Lord in a world that is often hostile to God and his values.

1. **Children (and Parents) Are Never Too Young (or Too Old) to Learn about God**
   Teaching your children to love the Lord in their early years will help them stay true to the Lord later in life (see Proverbs 22:6). Conversely, parents are never too old to learn about God.
2. **Make Sure Your Children Hear the Gospel Message** The gospel must first be preached in the home (see Acts 16:29-34). This might include sharing the Good News with your parents.
3. **Encourage Your Children's Spiritual Growth** As the apostle Paul suggests, a loving father encourages his children to live a life pleasing to God (see 1 Thessalonians 2:11-12).
4. **Watch the Legacy You Leave** Your devotion to God—or lack of it—will make a resounding impression on the next generation (see 2 Chronicles 17:3-6).
5. **Discipline Your Children** Parents who love their children and want them to grow up into young men and women of character will discipline them (see Proverbs 29:15).
6. **Avoid Provoking Your Children** Your discipline must be tempered with love so that your children do not become resentful (see Ephesians 6:1-4).

How Do I Know I'm Saved?

The Bible says that when you believe in Jesus and accept him into your life, you can be sure you have eternal life (see John 10:27-29). You may not feel any different, but you have been washed clean of your sin. And just as a shepherd protects his sheep, Jesus protects us from eternal harm. When you follow Jesus by believing and obeying him, he gives you everlasting life (see Hebrews 5:9). God gives you good gifts, and he does not take them away. Your salvation is a gift from God (see Ephesians 2:8-9).

Share Your Faith

Next to personally knowing Jesus and walking with him, one of the greatest blessings of the Christian life is to actually lead someone to Jesus Christ. The good news is that God wants to use you—not just pastors, missionaries, and evangelists—as his instrument to speak to others.

Jesus gave us this very commission in Mark 16:15, where he says, "Go into all the world and preach the Good News to everyone, everywhere." This wonderful charge is known as the "great commission." But the way some Christians follow it, you would think it was the "great suggestion." Sharing our faith, however, is something that Jesus wants—and commands—us to do! How do we do this? First Peter 3:15-16 tells us to be ready to give an answer to anyone who asks us about the hope we have in Jesus. Here are four passages from God's Word that will help you to share your faith.

1. **You Don't Need Any Training to Share.** A changed heart is all you need to begin sharing your faith with others (see John 9:1-41, p. 903).
2. **Be Open to God's Leading.** Effectively sharing your faith begins with a willing heart (see Acts 8:4-8, 26-38, p. 933).
3. **Understand the Simplicity of the Gospel.** The message of the gospel is simple yet powerful (see 1 Corinthians 2:1-5, p. 985).
4. **Share Your Own Story.** Never underestimate the strength of your personal testimony (see Acts 26:1-23, p. 957).

Have you ever opened your Bible and asked the following:

- What does this passage really mean?
- How does it apply to my life?
- Why does some of the Bible seem irrelevant?
- What do these ancient cultures have to do with today?
- I love God; why can't I understand what he is saying to me through his Word?
- What's going on in the lives of these Bible people?

Many Christians do not read the Bible regularly. Why? Because in the pressures of daily living they cannot find a connection between the timeless principles of Scripture and the ever-present problems of day-by-day living.

Applying God's Word is a vital part of one's relationship with God; it is the evidence that we are obeying him. The difficulty in applying the Bible is not with the Bible itself, but with the reader's inability to bridge the gap between the past and the present, the conceptual and the practical. When we don't or can't do this, spiritual dryness, shallowness, and indifference are the results. The words of Scripture itself cry out to us: "And remember, it is a message to obey, not just to listen to. If you don't obey, you are only fooling yourself" (James 1:22).

The *Life Application Study Bible* does what a good resource Bible should do—it helps you understand the context of a passage, gives important background and historical information, explains difficult words and phrases, and helps you see the interrelationships within Scripture. But it does much more. The *Life Application Study Bible* goes deeper into God's Word, helping you discover the timeless truth being communicated, see the relevance for your life, and make a personal application. While some study Bibles attempt application, over 75 percent of this Bible is application oriented. The notes answer the questions "So what?" and "What does this passage mean to me, my family, my friends, my job, my neighborhood, my church, my country?"

Imagine reading a familiar passage of Scripture and gaining fresh insight, as if it were the first time you had ever read it. How much richer your life would be if you left each Bible reading with a new perspective and a small change for the better. A small change every day adds up to a changed life—and that is the very purpose of Scripture.

This edition of the Gospel of John includes a special section (pages vi–xvi) adapted from the *New Believer's Bible.* This study material for new believers was written by Greg Laurie, an evangelist who holds Harvest Crusades in major cities across the United States.

The complete *Life Application Study Bible,* New Living Translation edition, will be available in October 1996. The *New Believer's Bible* will be available in November 1996.

JOHN

VITAL STATISTICS

PURPOSE:
To prove conclusively that Jesus is the Son of God and that all who believe in him will have eternal life

AUTHOR:
John the apostle, son of Zebedee, brother of James, called a "Son of Thunder"

TO WHOM WRITTEN:
New Christians and searching non-Christians

DATE WRITTEN:
Probably A.D. 85–90

SETTING:
Written after the destruction of Jerusalem in A.D. 70 and before John's exile to the island of Patmos

KEY VERSES:
"Jesus' disciples saw him do many other miraculous signs besides the ones recorded in this book. But these are written so that you may believe that Jesus is the Messiah, the Son of God, and that by believing in him you will have life" (20:30, 31).

KEY PEOPLE:
Jesus, John the Baptist, the disciples, Mary, Martha, Lazarus, Jesus' mother, Pilate, Mary Magdalene

KEY PLACES:
Judean countryside, Samaria, Galilee, Bethany, Jerusalem

SPECIAL FEATURES:
Of the eight miracles recorded, six are unique (among the Gospels) to John, as is the "Upper Room Discourse" (chapters 14—17). Over 90 percent of John is unique to his Gospel— John does not contain a genealogy or any record of Jesus' birth, childhood, temptation, transfiguration, appointment of the disciples, nor any account of Jesus' parables, ascension, or great commission.

HE SPOKE, and galaxies whirled into place, stars burned the heavens, and planets began orbiting their suns—words of awesome, unlimited, unleashed power. He spoke again, and the waters and lands were filled with plants and creatures, running, swimming, growing, and multiplying— words of animating, breathing, pulsing life. Again he spoke, and man and woman were formed, thinking, speaking, and loving—words of personal and creative glory. Eternal, infinite, unlimited—he was, is, and always will be the Maker and Lord of all that exists.

And then he came in the flesh to a speck in the universe called planet Earth. The mighty Creator became a part of the creation, limited by time and space and susceptible to aging, sickness, and death. But love propelled him, and so he came to rescue and save those who were lost and to give them the gift of eternity. He is the Word; he is Jesus, the Messiah.

It is this truth that the apostle John brings to us in this book. John's Gospel is not a life of Christ; it is a powerful argument for the incarnation, a conclusive demonstration that Jesus was, and is, the very heaven-sent Son of God and the only source of eternal life.

John discloses Jesus' identity with his very first words, "In the beginning the Word already existed. He was with God, and he was God. He was in the beginning with God" (1:1, 2); and the rest of the book continues the theme. John, the eyewitness, chose eight of Jesus' miracles (or miraculous signs, as he calls them) to reveal his divine/human nature and his life-giving mission. These signs are (1) turning water to wine (2:1–11), (2) healing the official's son (4:46–54), (3) healing the lame man at the Pool of Bethesda (5:1–9), (4) feeding the 5,000 with just a few loaves and fish (6:1–14), (5) walking on the water (6:15–21), (6) restoring sight to the blind man (9:1–41), (7) raising Lazarus from the dead (11:1–44), and, after the Resurrection, (8) giving the disciples an overwhelming catch of fish (21:1–14).

In every chapter Jesus' deity is revealed. And Jesus' true identity is underscored through the titles he is given—the Word, the only Son, Lamb of God, Son of God, true bread, life, resurrection, vine. And the formula is "I am." When Jesus uses this phrase, he affirms his preexistence and eternal deity. Jesus says, *I am* the bread of life (6:35); *I am* the light of the world (8:12; 9:5); *I am* the gate (10:7); *I am* the good shepherd (10:11, 14); *I am* the resurrection and the life (11:25); *I am* the way, the truth, and the life (14:6); and *I am* the true vine (15:1).

The greatest sign, of course, is the Resurrection, and John provides a stirring eyewitness account of finding the empty tomb. Then he records various post-Resurrection appearances by Jesus.

John, the devoted follower of Christ, has given us a personal and powerful look at Jesus Christ, the eternal Son of God. As you read his story, commit yourself to believe in and follow him.

Tiberius Caesar becomes emperor 14		Pontius Pilate appointed governor 26	Jesus begins his ministry 26/27	Jesus and Nicodemus 27	Jesus chooses twelve disciples 28	Jesus feeds 5,000 29	Jesus is crucified, rises again, and ascends 30

THE BLUEPRINT

A. BIRTH AND PREPARATION OF JESUS, THE SON OF GOD (1:1—2:12)

John makes it clear that Jesus is not just a man; he is the eternal Son of God. He is the light of the world because he offers this gift of eternal life to all people. How blind and foolish to call Jesus nothing more than an unusually good man or moral teacher. Yet we sometimes act as if this were true when we casually toss around his words and go about living our own way. If Jesus is the eternal Son of God, we should pay attention to his divine identity and life-giving message.

B. MESSAGE AND MINISTRY OF JESUS, THE SON OF GOD (2:13—12:50)
1. Jesus encounters belief and unbelief from the people
2. Jesus encounters conflict with the religious leaders
3. Jesus encounters crucial events in Jerusalem

Jesus meets with individuals, preaches to great crowds, trains his disciples, and debates with the religious leaders. The message that he is the Son of God receives a mixed reaction. Some worship him, some are puzzled, some shrink back, and some move to silence him. We see the same varied reactions today. Times have changed, but people's hearts remain hard. May we see ourselves in these encounters Jesus had with people, and may our response be to worship and follow him.

C. DEATH AND RESURRECTION OF JESUS, THE SON OF GOD (13:1—21:25)
1. Jesus teaches his disciples
2. Jesus completes his mission

Jesus carefully instructed the disciples how to continue to believe even after his death, yet they could not take it in. After he died and the first reports came back that Jesus was alive, the disciples could not believe it. Thomas is especially remembered as one who refused to believe even when he heard the eyewitness accounts from other disciples. May we not be like Thomas, demanding a physical face-to-face encounter, but may we accept the eyewitness testimony of the disciples that John has recorded in this Gospel.

MEGATHEMES

THEME	EXPLANATION	IMPORTANCE
Jesus Christ, Son of God	John shows us that Jesus is unique as God's special Son, yet he is fully God. Because he is fully God, Jesus is able to reveal God to us clearly and accurately.	Because Jesus is God's Son, we can perfectly trust what he says. By trusting him, we can gain an open mind to understand God's message and fulfill his purpose in our lives.
Eternal Life	Because Jesus is God, he lives forever. Before the world began, he lived with God, and he will reign forever with him. In John we see Jesus revealed in power and magnificence even before his resurrection.	Jesus offers eternal life to us. We are invited to begin living in a personal, eternal relationship with him now. Although we must grow old and die, by trusting him we can have a new life that lasts forever.
Belief	John records eight specific signs, or miracles, that show the nature of Jesus' power and love. We see his power over everything created, and we see his love of all people. These signs encourage us to believe in him.	Believing is active, living, and continuous trust in Jesus as God. When we believe in his life, his words, his death, and his resurrection, we are cleansed from sin and receive power to follow him. But we must respond to him by believing.
Holy Spirit	Jesus taught his disciples that the Holy Spirit would come after he ascended from earth. The Holy Spirit would then indwell, guide, counsel, and comfort those who follow Jesus. Through the Holy Spirit, Christ's presence and power are multiplied in all who believe.	Through God's Holy Spirit, we are drawn to him in faith. We must know the Holy Spirit to understand all Jesus taught. We can experience Jesus' love and guidance as we allow the Holy Spirit to do his work in us.

Resurrection   On the third day after he died, Jesus rose from the dead. This was verified by his disciples and many eyewitnesses. This reality changed the disciples from frightened deserters to dynamic leaders in the new church. This fact is the foundation of the Christian faith.

We can be changed as the disciples were and have confidence that our bodies will one day be raised to live with Christ forever. The same power that raised Christ to life can give us the ability to follow Christ each day.

KEY PLACES IN JOHN

John's story begins as John the Baptist ministers near Bethany east of the Jordan (1:28ff). Jesus also begins his ministry, talking to some of the men who would later become his 12 disciples. Jesus' ministry in Galilee began with a visit to a wedding in Cana (2:1ff). Then he went to Capernaum, which became his new home (2:12). He journeyed to Jerusalem for the special festivals (2:13) and there met with Nicodemus, a religious leader (3:1ff). When Jesus left Judea, he traveled through Samaria and ministered to the Samaritans (4:1ff). Jesus did miracles in Galilee (4:46ff) and in Judea and Jerusalem (5:1ff). We follow him as he fed 5,000 near Bethsaida beside the Sea of Galilee (Sea of Tiberias) (6:1ff), walked on the water to his frightened disciples (6:16ff), preached through Galilee (7:1), returned to Jerusalem (7:2ff), preached beyond the Jordan in Perea (10:40), raised Lazarus from the dead in Bethany (11:1ff), and finally entered Jerusalem for the last time to celebrate the Passover with his disciples and give them key teachings about what was to come and how they should act. His last hours before his crucifixion were spent in the city (13:1ff), in a grove of olive trees (the Garden of Gethsemane) (18:1ff), and finally in various buildings in Jerusalem during his trial (18:12ff). He would be crucified, but he would rise again as he had promised.

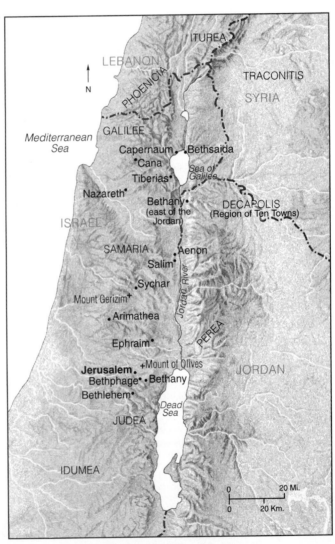

The broken lines (—·—·) indicate modern boundaries.

A. BIRTH AND PREPARATION OF JESUS, THE SON OF GOD (1:1—2:12)

In this Gospel, John provides clear evidence that Jesus is the Son of God and that by believing in him we may have eternal life. John also provides unique material about Jesus' birth. He did not come into being when he was born, because he is eternal.

God Became a Human (**2**)

1:1
Gen 1:1
Phil 2:6
1 Jn 5:21

1:3
1 Cor 8:6
Col 1:16-17
Heb 1:2

1:4
John 3:15-16, 36;
6:35, 48; 8:12;
1 Jn 5:12, 20

1:9
1 Jn 2:8

1 In the beginning the Word already existed. He was with God, and he was God. ²He was in the beginning with God. ³He created everything there is. Nothing exists that he didn't make. ⁴Life itself was in him, and this life gives light to everyone. ⁵The light shines through the darkness, and the darkness can never extinguish it.

⁶God sent John the Baptist ⁷to tell everyone about the light so that everyone might believe because of his testimony. ⁸John himself was not the light; he was only a witness to the light. ⁹The one who is the true light, who gives light to everyone, was going to come into the world.

¹⁰But although the world was made through him, the world didn't recognize him when he came. ¹¹Even in his own land and among his own people, he was not accepted. ¹²But

1:1 What Jesus taught and what he did are tied inseparably to who he is. John shows Jesus as fully human and fully God. Although Jesus took upon himself full humanity and lived as a man, he never ceased to be the eternal God who has always existed, the Creator and Sustainer of all things, and the source of eternal life. This is the truth about Jesus, and the foundation of all truth. If we cannot or do not believe this basic truth, we will not have enough faith to trust our eternal destiny to him. That is why John wrote this Gospel—to build faith and confidence in Jesus Christ so that we may believe that he truly was and is the Son of God (20:30, 31).

1:1 John wrote to believers everywhere, both Jews and non-Jews (Gentiles). As one of Jesus' 12 disciples, John was an eyewitness so his story is accurate. His book is not a biography (like the book of Luke); it is a thematic presentation of Jesus' life. Many in John's original audience had a Greek background. Greek culture encouraged worship of many mythological gods, whose supernatural characteristics were as important to Greeks as genealogies were to Jews. John shows that Jesus is not only different from but superior to these gods of mythology.

1:1ff What does John mean by "the Word"? *The Word* was a term used by theologians and philosophers, both Jews and Greeks, in many different ways. In Hebrew Scripture, *the Word* was an agent of creation (Psalm 33:6), the source of God's message to his people through the prophets (Hosea 4:1), and God's law, his standard of holiness (Psalm 119:11). In Greek philosophy, *the Word* was the principle of reason that governed the world, or the thought still in the mind, while in Hebrew thought, *the Word* was another expression for God. John's description shows clearly that he is speaking of Jesus (see especially 1:14)—a human being he knew and loved, but at the same time the Creator of the universe, the ultimate revelation of God, the living picture of God's holiness, the one who "holds all creation together" (Colossians 1:17). To Jewish readers, to say this man Jesus "was God" was blasphemous. To Greek readers, "the Word became human" (1:14) was unthinkable. To John, this new understanding of the Word was the Good News of Jesus Christ.

1:3 When God created, he made something from nothing. Because we are created beings, we have no basis for pride. Remember that you exist only because God made you, and you have special gifts only because God gave them to you. With God you are something valuable and unique; apart from God you are nothing, and if you try to live without him, you will be abandoning the purpose for which you were made.

1:3-5 Do you ever feel that your life is too complex for God to understand? Remember, God created the entire universe, and nothing is too difficult for him. God created you; he is alive today, and his love is bigger than any problem you may face.

1:4, 5 "The darkness can never extinguish it" means the darkness of evil never has and never will overcome God's light. Jesus Christ is the Creator of life, and his life brings light to humankind. In his light, we see ourselves as we really are (sinners in need of a Savior). When we follow Jesus, the true Light, we can avoid walking blindly and falling into sin. He lights the path ahead of us so we can see how to live. He removes the darkness of sin from our lives. Have you allowed the light of Christ to shine into your life? Let Christ guide your life, and you'll never need to stumble in darkness.

1:6-8 For more information on John the Baptist, see his Profile in this chapter.

1:8 We, like John the Baptist, are not the source of God's light; we merely reflect that light. Jesus Christ is the true Light; he helps us see our way to God and shows us how to walk along that way. But Christ has chosen to reflect his light through his followers to an unbelieving world, perhaps because unbelievers are not able to bear the full blazing glory of his light firsthand. The word *witness* indicates our role as reflectors of Christ's light. We are never to present ourselves as the light to others, but are always to point them to Christ, the Light.

1:10, 11 Although Christ created the world, the people he created didn't recognize him (1:10). Even the people chosen by God to prepare the rest of the world for the Messiah rejected him (1:11), although the entire Old Testament pointed to his coming.

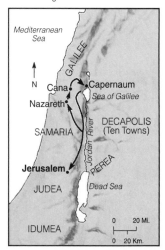

JESUS' FIRST TRAVELS After his baptism by John in the Jordan River and the temptation by Satan in the wilderness (see the map in Mark 1), Jesus returned to Galilee. He visited Nazareth, Cana, and Capernaum, and then returned to Jerusalem for the Passover.

to all who believed him and accepted him, he gave the right to become children of God. [1:12] Rom 8:15-16, 29; 1 Jn 3:1, 23
[13]They are reborn! This is not a physical birth resulting from human passion or plan—this rebirth comes from God.

[14]So the Word became human and lived here on earth among us. He was full of unfailing love and faithfulness.* And we have seen his glory, the glory of the only Son of the Father. [1:14] Rom 1:3; 8:3; Gal 4:4; Phil 2:6-8; Col 2:9; 1 Tim 3:16; Heb 2:14; 1 Jn 1:1; 4:2-3

[15]John pointed him out to the people. He shouted to the crowds, "This is the one I was talking about when I said, 'Someone is coming who is far greater than I am, for he existed long before I did.'" [1:16] Col 2:9-10

[16]We have all benefited from the rich blessings he brought to us—one gracious blessing after another.* [17]For the law was given through Moses; God's unfailing love and faithfulness came through Jesus Christ. [18]No one has ever seen God. But his only Son, who is himself God,* is near to the Father's heart; he has told us about him. [1:17] Exod 31:18; 34:28; John 7:19 / [1:18] Exod 33:20; 2 Cor 4:4, 6; Col 1:15

John the Baptist Declares His Mission (19)

[19]This was the testimony of John when the Jewish leaders sent priests and Temple assistants* from Jerusalem to ask John whether he claimed to be the Messiah. [20]He flatly denied it. "I am not the Messiah," he said. [1:19-28] //Matt 3:1-12; //Mark 1:2-8; //Luke 3:1-16 / [1:20] Luke 3:15; John 3:28

[21]"Well then, who are you?" they asked. "Are you Elijah?"

"No," he replied.

"Are you the Prophet?"*

"No." [1:21] Deut 18:15; Mal 4:5; Matt 11:14

[22]"Then who are you? Tell us, so we can give an answer to those who sent us. What do you have to say about yourself?"

1:14 Greek *grace and truth;* also in 1:17.   1:16 Greek *grace upon grace.*   1:18 Some manuscripts read *his one and only Son.*   1:19 Greek *and Levites.*   1:21 See Deut 18:15, 18; Mal 4:5-6.

1:12, 13 All who welcome Jesus Christ as Lord of their lives are reborn spiritually, receiving new life from God. Through faith in Christ, this new birth changes us from the inside out—rearranging our attitudes, desires, and motives. Being born makes you physically alive and places you in your parents' family (1:13). Being born of God makes you spiritually alive and puts you in God's family (1:12). Have you asked Christ to make you a new person? This fresh start in life is available to all who believe in Christ.

1:14 "The Word became human." By doing so, Christ became (1) *the perfect teacher*—in Jesus' life we see how God thinks and therefore how we should think (Philippians 2:5-11); (2) *the perfect example*—as a model of what we are to become, he shows us how to live and gives us the power to live that way (1 Peter 2:21); (3) *the perfect sacrifice*—Jesus came as a sacrifice for all sins, and his death satisfied God's requirements for the removal of sin (Colossians 1:15-23).

1:14 "The only Son of the Father" means Jesus is God's only and unique Son. The emphasis is on *unique.* Jesus is one of a kind and enjoys a relationship with God. He is unlike all believers, who are called "children of God."

1:14 When Jesus was born, God became a man. He was not part man and part God; he was completely human and completely divine (Colossians 2:9). Before Christ came, people could know God partially. After Christ came, people could know God fully because he became visible and tangible in Christ. Christ is the perfect expression of God in human form. The two most common errors people make about Jesus are to minimize his humanity or to minimize his divinity. Jesus is both God and man.

1:17 Law and grace ("God's unfailing love and faithfulness") are both aspects of God's nature that he uses in dealing with us. Moses emphasized God's law and justice, while Jesus Christ came to highlight God's mercy, love, faithfulness, and forgiveness. Moses could only be the giver of the law, while Christ came to fulfill

the law (Matthew 5:17). The nature and will of God were revealed in the law; now the nature and will of God are revealed in Jesus Christ. Rather than coming through cold stone tablets, God's revelation now comes through a person's life. As we get to know Christ better, our understanding of God will increase.

1:18 God communicated through various people in the Old Testament, usually prophets who were told to give specific messages. But no one ever *saw* God. Jesus is both God and the Father's unique Son. In Christ, God revealed his nature and essence in a way that could be seen and touched. In Christ, God became a man who lived on earth.

1:19 The priests and Temple assistants (also called Levites) were respected religious leaders in Jerusalem. Priests served in the Temple, and Temple assistants helped them. The Pharisees (1:24) were a group that both John the Baptist and Jesus often denounced. Many of them outwardly obeyed God's laws to look pious, while inwardly their hearts were filled with pride and greed. The Pharisees believed that their own oral traditions were just as important as God's inspired Word. For more information on the Pharisees, see the charts in Matthew 3 and Mark 2.

These leaders came to see John the Baptist for several reasons: (1) Their duty as guardians of the faith caused them to want to investigate any new preaching (Deuteronomy 13:1-5; 18:20-22). (2) They wanted to find out if John had the credentials of a prophet. (3) John had quite a following, and it was growing. They were probably jealous and wanted to see why this man was so popular.

1:21-23 In the religious leaders' minds, there were four options regarding John the Baptist's identity: He was (1) the Prophet foretold by Moses (Deuteronomy 18:15), (2) Elijah (Malachi 4:5), (3) the Messiah, or (4) a false prophet. John denied being the first three personages. Instead, he called himself, in the words of the Old Testament prophet Isaiah, "The voice of someone shouting, 'Make a highway for the LORD through the wilderness. Make a straight, smooth road through the desert for our God'" (Isaiah

1:23
†Isa 40:3

23 John replied in the words of Isaiah:

"I am a voice shouting in the wilderness,
'Prepare a straight pathway for the Lord's coming!'"*

1:26
Mal 3:1
Matt 3:11
Mark 1:8
Luke 3:16

24 Then those who were sent by the Pharisees 25 asked him, "If you aren't the Messiah or Elijah or the Prophet, what right do you have to baptize?"

1:27
Mark 1:7
John 1:15
Acts 13:25

26 John told them, "I baptize with* water, but right here in the crowd is someone you do not know, 27 who will soon begin his ministry. I am not even worthy to be his slave.*"

1:23 Isa 40:3.   **1:26** Or *in;* also in 1:31, 33.   **1:27** Greek *to untie his sandals.*

JOHN THE BAPTIST

There's no getting around it—John the Baptist was unique. He wore odd clothes and ate strange food and preached an unusual message to the Judeans who went out to the wastelands to see him.

But John did not aim at uniqueness for its own sake. Instead, he aimed at obedience. He knew he had a specific role to play in the world—announcing the coming of the Savior—and he put all his energies into this task. Luke tells us that John was in the wilderness when God's word of direction came to him. John was ready and waiting. The angel who had announced John's birth to Zechariah had made it clear this child was to be a Nazirite—one set apart for God's service. John remained faithful to that calling.

This wild-looking man had no power or position in the Jewish political system, but he spoke with almost irresistible authority. People were moved by his words because he spoke the truth, challenging them to turn from their sins and baptizing them as a symbol of their repentance. They responded by the hundreds. But even as people crowded to him, he pointed beyond himself, never forgetting that his main role was to announce the coming of the Savior.

The words of truth that moved many to repentance goaded others to resistance and resentment. John even challenged Herod to admit his sin. Herodias, the woman Herod had married illegally, decided to get rid of this wilderness preacher. Although she was able to have him killed, she was not able to stop his message. The one John had announced was already on the move. John had accomplished his mission.

God has given each of us a purpose for living, and we can trust him to guide us. John did not have the complete Bible as we know it today, but he focused his life on the truth he knew from the available Old Testament Scriptures. Likewise, we can discover in God's Word the truths he wants us to know. And as these truths work in us, others will be drawn to him. God can use you in a way he can use no one else. Let him know your willingness to follow him today.

Strengths and accomplishments	• The God-appointed messenger to announce the arrival of Jesus • A preacher whose theme was repentance • A fearless confronter • Known for his remarkable life-style • Uncompromising
Lessons from his life	• God does not guarantee an easy or safe life to those who serve him • Doing what God desires is the greatest possible life investment • Standing for the truth is more important than life itself
Vital statistics	• Where: Judea • Occupation: Prophet • Relatives: Father: Zechariah. Mother: Elizabeth. Distant relative: Jesus • Contemporaries: Herod, Herodias
Key verse	"I assure you, of all who have ever lived, none is greater than John the Baptist. Yet even the most insignificant person in the Kingdom of Heaven is greater than he is!" (Matthew 11:11).

John's story is told in all four Gospels. His coming was predicted in Isaiah 40:3 and Malachi 4:5; and he is mentioned in Acts 1:5, 22; 10:37; 11:16; 13:24, 25; 18:25; 19:3, 4.

40:3). The leaders kept pressing John to say who he was because people were expecting the Messiah to come (Luke 3:15). But John emphasized only *why* he had come—to prepare the way for the Messiah. The Pharisees missed the point. They wanted to know who John was, but John wanted them to know who Jesus was.

1:25, 26 John was baptizing Jews. The Essenes (a strict, monastic sect of Judaism) practiced baptism for purification, but normally only non-Jews (Gentiles) were baptized when they converted to Judaism. When the Pharisees questioned John's authority to baptize, they were asking who gave John the right to treat God's chosen people like Gentiles. John said, "I baptize with water"—he was merely helping the people perform a symbolic act of repentance. But soon one would come who would truly *forgive* sins, something only the Son of God—the Messiah—could do.

1:27 John the Baptist said he was not even worthy to be Christ's slave. But according to Luke 7:28, Jesus said that John was the greatest of all prophets. If such a great person felt inadequate even to be Christ's slave, how much more should we lay aside our pride to serve Christ! When we truly understand who Christ is, our pride and self-importance melt away.

28 This incident took place at Bethany, a village east of the Jordan River, where John was baptizing.

John the Baptist Proclaims Jesus as the Messiah (20)

29 The next day John saw Jesus coming toward him and said, "Look! There is the Lamb of God who takes away the sin of the world! 30 He is the one I was talking about when I said, 'Soon a man is coming who is far greater than I am, for he existed long before I did.' 31 I didn't know he was the one, but I have been baptizing with water in order to point him out to Israel."

32 Then John said, "I saw the Holy Spirit descending like a dove from heaven and resting upon him. 33 I didn't know he was the one, but when God sent me to baptize with water, he told me, 'When you see the Holy Spirit descending and resting upon someone, he is the one you are looking for. He is the one who baptizes with the Holy Spirit.' 34 I saw this happen to Jesus, so I testify that he is the Son of God.*"

The First Disciples Follow Jesus (21)

35 The following day, John was again standing with two of his disciples. 36 As Jesus walked by, John looked at him and then declared, "Look! There is the Lamb of God!" 37 Then John's two disciples turned and followed Jesus.

38 Jesus looked around and saw them following. "What do you want?" he asked them.

They replied, "Rabbi" (which means Teacher), "where are you staying?"

39 "Come and see," he said. It was about four o'clock in the afternoon when they went with him to the place, and they stayed there the rest of the day.

40 Andrew, Simon Peter's brother, was one of these men who had heard what John said and then followed Jesus. 41 The first thing Andrew did was to find his brother, Simon, and tell him, "We have found the Messiah" (which means the Christ).

1:34 Some manuscripts read *the chosen One of God.*

1:28 John 3:26; 10:40

1:29 Isa 53:7 / 1 Cor 5:7 / 1 Pet 1:19

1:32 Matt 3:16 / Mark 1:10 / Luke 3:22

1:33 Luke 3:16 / Acts 1:5

1:34 John 1:49; 10:36

1:40 Matt 4:18-22 / Mark 1:16 / Luke 5:2-11

1:41 Ps 2:2 / John 4:25

1:29 Every morning and evening, a lamb was sacrificed in the Temple for the sins of the people (Exodus 29:38-42). Isaiah 53:7 prophesied that the Messiah, God's servant, would be led to the slaughter like a lamb. To pay the penalty for sin, a life had to be given—and God chose to provide the sacrifice himself. The sins of the world were removed when Jesus died as the perfect sacrifice. This is the way our sins are forgiven (1 Corinthians 5:7). The "sin of the world" means everyone's sin, the sin of each individual. Jesus paid the price of *your* sin by his death. You can receive forgiveness by confessing your sin to him and asking for his forgiveness.

1:30 Although John the Baptist was a well-known preacher who attracted large crowds, he was content for Jesus to take the higher place. This is true humility, the basis for greatness in preaching, teaching, or any other work we do for Christ. When you are content to do what God wants you to do and let Jesus Christ be honored for it, God will do great things through you.

1:31-34 At Jesus' baptism, John the Baptist had declared Jesus to be the Messiah. At that time God had given John a sign to show him that Jesus truly had been sent from God (1:33). John and Jesus were related (see Luke 1:36), so John probably knew who he was. But it wasn't until Jesus' baptism that John understood that Jesus was the Messiah. Jesus' baptism is described in Matthew 3:13-17; Mark 1:9-11; and Luke 3:21, 22.

1:33 John the Baptist's baptism with water was preparatory, because it was for repentance and symbolized the washing away of sins. Jesus, by contrast, would baptize with the Holy Spirit. He would send the Holy Spirit upon all believers, empowering them to live and to teach the message of salvation. This outpouring of the Spirit came after Jesus had risen from the dead and ascended into heaven (see 20:22; Acts 2).

1:34 John the Baptist's job was to point people to Jesus, their long-awaited Messiah. Today people are looking for someone to give them security in an insecure world. Our job is to point them to Christ and to show that he is the one whom they seek.

1:35ff These new disciples used several names for Jesus: Lamb of God (1:36), Rabbi (1:38), Messiah (1:41), Son of God (1:49), and King of Israel (1:49). As they got to know Jesus, their appreciation for him grew. The more time we spend getting to know Christ, the more we will understand and appreciate who he is. We may be drawn to him for his teaching, but we will come to know him as the Son of God. Although these disciples made this verbal shift in a few days, they would not fully understand Jesus until three years later (Acts 2). What they so easily professed had to be worked out in experience. We may find that words of faith come easily, but deep appreciation for Christ comes with living by faith.

1:37 One of the two disciples was Andrew (1:40). The other was probably John, the writer of this book. Why did these disciples leave John the Baptist? Because that's what John wanted them to do—he was pointing the way to Jesus, the one John had prepared them to follow. These were Jesus' first disciples, along with Simon Peter (1:42) and Nathanael (1:45).

1:38 When the two disciples began to follow Jesus, he asked them, "What do you want?" Following Christ is not enough; we must follow him for the right reasons. To follow Christ for our own purposes would be asking Christ to follow us—to align with us to support and advance our cause, not his. We must examine our motives for following him. Are we seeking his glory or ours?

1:40-42 Andrew accepted John the Baptist's testimony about Jesus and immediately went to tell his brother, Simon, about him. There was no question in Andrew's mind that Jesus was the Messiah. Not only did he tell his brother, but he was also eager to introduce others to Jesus (see 6:8, 9; 12:22).

1:42
Matt 16:18
1 Cor 15:5
1 Pet 2:5

⁴²Then Andrew brought Simon to meet Jesus. Looking intently at Simon, Jesus said, "You are Simon, the son of John—but you will be called Cephas" (which means Peter*).

1:43
John 6:5-6;
12:20-22

⁴³The next day Jesus decided to go to Galilee. He found Philip and said to him, "Come, be my disciple." ⁴⁴Philip was from Bethsaida, Andrew and Peter's hometown.

1:45
Gen 3:15
Num 21:8-9; 24:17
Deut 18:15, 18
Isa 7:14; 11:1-10;
52:10, 13; 53:1-12
Jer 23:5-6; 30:9
Ezek 34:23-24;
37:24-25
Hos 11:1
Mic 5:2
Zech 3:8-9;
6:12-13; 9:9
Mal 3:1; 4:2, 5

⁴⁵Philip went off to look for Nathanael and told him, "We have found the very person Moses and the prophets wrote about! His name is Jesus, the son of Joseph from Nazareth."

⁴⁶"Nazareth!" exclaimed Nathanael. "Can anything good come from there?"

"Just come and see for yourself," Philip said.

⁴⁷As they approached, Jesus said, "Here comes an honest man—a true son of Israel."

⁴⁸"How do you know about me?" Nathanael asked.

And Jesus replied, "I could see you under the fig tree before Philip found you."

1:49
2 Sam 7:14
Ps 2:2
John 1:34; 20:31

⁴⁹Nathanael replied, "Teacher, you are the Son of God—the King of Israel!"

⁵⁰Jesus asked him, "Do you believe all this just because I told you I had seen you under the fig tree? You will see greater things than this." ⁵¹Then he said, "The truth is,

1:51
Gen 28:12

you will all see heaven open and the angels of God going up and down upon the Son of Man."*

Jesus Turns Water into Wine (22)

2:1
John 1:35, 43

2 The next day* Jesus' mother was a guest at a wedding celebration in the village of Cana in Galilee. ²Jesus and his disciples were also invited to the celebration. ³The wine supply ran out during the festivities, so Jesus' mother spoke to him about the problem. "They have no more wine," she told him.

2:4
John 7:30; 8:20

⁴"How does that concern you and me?" Jesus asked. "My time has not yet come."

⁵But his mother told the servants, "Do whatever he tells you."

1:42 The names *Cephas* and *Peter* both mean "rock."   **1:51** See Gen 28:10-17, the account of Jacob's ladder.
2:1 Greek *On the third day;* see 1:35, 43.

1:42   Jesus saw not only who Simon was, but who he would become. That is why he gave him a new name—*Cephas* in Aramaic, *Peter* in Greek (the name means "a rock"). Peter is not presented as rock-solid throughout the Gospels, but he became a solid rock in the days of the early church, as we learn in the book of Acts. By giving Simon a new name, Jesus introduced a change in character. For more on Simon Peter, see his Profile in Matthew 27.

1:46   Nazareth was despised by the Jews because a Roman army garrison was located there. Some have speculated that an aloof attitude or a poor reputation in morals and religion on the part of the people of Nazareth led to Nathanael's harsh comment. Nathanael's hometown was Cana, about four miles from Nazareth.

1:46   When Nathanael heard that the Messiah was from Nazareth, he was surprised. Philip responded, "Come and see for yourself." Fortunately for Nathanael, he went to meet Jesus and became a disciple. If he had stuck to his prejudice without investigating further, he would have missed the Messiah! Don't let people's stereotypes about Christ cause them to miss his power and love. Invite them to come and see who Jesus really is.

1:47-49   Jesus knew about Nathanael before the two ever met. Jesus also knows what we are really like. An honest person will feel comfortable with the thought that Jesus knows him or her through and through. A dishonest person will feel uncomfortable. You can't pretend to be something you're not. God knows the real you and wants *you* to follow him.

1:51   This is a reference to Jacob's dream recorded in Genesis 28:12. As the unique God-man, Jesus would be the ladder between heaven and earth. Jesus is not saying that this would be a physical experience (that they would see the ladder with their eyes) like the Transfiguration, but that they would have spiritual insight into Jesus' true nature and purpose for coming.

2:1, 2   Jesus was on a mission to save the world, the greatest mission in the history of humankind. Yet he took time to attend a

wedding and take part in its festivities. We may be tempted to think we should not take time out from our "important" work for social occasions. But maybe these social occasions are part of our mission. Jesus valued these wedding festivities because they involved people, and Jesus came to be with people. Our mission can often be accomplished in joyous times of celebration with others. Bring balance to your life by bringing Jesus into times of pleasure as well as times of work.

2:1-3   Weddings in Jesus' day were week-long festivals. Banquets would be prepared for many guests, and the week would be spent celebrating the new life of the married couple. Often the whole town was invited, and everybody would come—it was considered an insult to refuse an invitation to a wedding. To accommodate many people, careful planning was needed. To run out of wine was more than embarrassing; it broke the strong unwritten laws of hospitality. Jesus was about to respond to a heartfelt need.

2:4   Mary was probably not asking Jesus to do a miracle; she was simply hoping that her son would help solve this major problem and find some wine. Tradition says that Joseph, Mary's husband, was dead, so she probably was used to asking for her son's help in certain situations. Jesus' answer to Mary is difficult to understand, but maybe that is the point. Although Mary did not understand what Jesus was going to do, she trusted him to do what was right. Those who believe in Jesus but run into situations they cannot understand must continue to trust that he will work in the best way.

2:5   Mary submitted to Jesus' way of doing things. She recognized that Jesus was more than her human son—he was the Son of God. When we bring our problems to Christ, we may think we know how he should take care of them. But he may have a completely different plan. Like Mary, we should submit and allow him to deal with the problem as he sees best.

[6]Six stone waterpots were standing there; they were used for Jewish ceremonial purposes and held twenty to thirty gallons* each. [7]Jesus told the servants, "Fill the jars with water." When the jars had been filled to the brim, [8]he said, "Dip some out and take it to the master of ceremonies." So they followed his instructions.

2:6
Mark 7:3-4
John 3:25

[9]When the master of ceremonies tasted the water that was now wine, not knowing where it had come from (though, of course, the servants knew), he called the bridegroom over. [10]"Usually a host serves the best wine first," he said. "Then, when everyone is full and doesn't care, he brings out the less expensive wines. But you have kept the best until now!"

2:9
John 4:46

[11]This miraculous sign at Cana in Galilee was Jesus' first display of his glory. And his disciples believed in him.

2:11
John 2:23; 3:2;
4:54; 6:14; 11:47;
12:37

[12]After the wedding he went to Capernaum for a few days with his mother, his brothers, and his disciples.

2:12
Matt 12:46-50

B. MESSAGE AND MINISTRY OF JESUS, THE SON OF GOD (2:13—12:50)

John stresses the deity of Christ. He gives us eight miracles that serve as signs that Jesus is the Messiah. In this section he records Jesus describing himself as the bread of life, the water of life, the light of the world, the door, and the good shepherd. John provides teachings of Jesus found nowhere else. This is the most theological of the four Gospels.

1. Jesus encounters belief and unbelief from the people

Jesus Clears the Temple (**23**)

[13]It was time for the annual Passover celebration, and Jesus went to Jerusalem. [14]In the Temple area he saw merchants selling cattle, sheep, and doves for sacrifices; and he saw money changers behind their counters. [15]Jesus made a whip from some ropes and chased

2:13-22
//Matt 21:12-17
//Mark 11:15-19
//Luke 19:45-48

2:6 Greek *2 or 3 measures* [75 to 113 liters].

2:6 The six stone waterpots were normally used for ceremonial washing. When full, the pots would hold 20 to 30 gallons. According to the Jews' ceremonial law, people became symbolically unclean by touching objects of everyday life. Before eating, the Jews would pour water over their hands to cleanse themselves of any bad influences associated with what they had touched.

2:10 People look everywhere but to God for excitement and meaning. For some reason, they expect God to be dull and lifeless. Just as the wine Jesus made was the best, so life in him is better than life on our own. Why wait until everything else runs out before trying God? Why save the best until last?

2:11 When the disciples saw Jesus' miracle, they believed. The miracle showed his power over nature and revealed the way he would go about his ministry—helping others, speaking with authority, and being in personal touch with people.

2:11 Miracles are not merely superhuman events, but events that demonstrate God's power. Almost every miracle Jesus did was a renewal of fallen creation—restoring sight, making the lame walk, even restoring life to the dead. Believe in Christ not because he is a superman but because he is the God who continues his creation, even in those of us who are poor, weak, crippled, orphaned, blind, deaf, or with some other desperate need for re-creation.

2:12 Capernaum became Jesus' home base during his ministry in Galilee. Located on a major trade route, it was an important city in the region, with a Roman garrison and a customs station. At Capernaum, Matthew was called to be a disciple (Matthew 9:9). The city was also the home of several other disciples (Matthew 4:13-19) and a high-ranking government official (4:46). It had at least one major synagogue. Although Jesus made this city his base of operations in Galilee, he condemned it for the people's unbelief (Matthew 11:23; Luke 10:15).

2:13 The Passover celebration took place yearly at the Temple in Jerusalem. Every Jewish male was expected to make a pilgrimage to Jerusalem during this time (Deuteronomy 16:16). This was a week-long festival—the Passover was one day, and the Festival of Unleavened Bread lasted the rest of the week.

The entire week commemorated the freeing of the Jews from slavery in Egypt (Exodus 12:1-13).

2:13 Jerusalem was both the religious and the political seat of Palestine, and the place where the Messiah was expected to arrive. The Temple was located there, and many Jewish families from all over the world would travel to Jerusalem during the key festivals. The Temple was on an imposing site, a hill overlooking the city. Solomon had built the first Temple on this same site almost 1,000 years earlier (959 B.C.), but his Temple had been destroyed by the Babylonians (2 Kings 25). The Temple was rebuilt in 516 B.C., and Herod the Great had enlarged and remodeled it.

2:14 The Temple area was always crowded during Passover with thousands of out-of-town visitors. The religious leaders crowded it even further by allowing money changers and merchants to set up booths in the Court of the Gentiles. They rationalized this practice as a convenience for the worshipers and as a way to make money for Temple upkeep. But the religious leaders did not seem to care that the Court of the Gentiles was so full of merchants that foreigners found it difficult to worship. And worship was the main purpose for visiting the Temple. No wonder Jesus was angry!

2:14 The Temple tax had to be paid in local currency, so foreigners had to have their money changed. But the money changers often would charge exorbitant exchange rates. The people also were required to make sacrifices for sins. Because of the long journey, many could not bring their own animals. Some who brought animals would have them rejected for imperfections. So animal merchants would do a flourishing business in the Temple courtyard. The price of sacrificial animals was much higher in the Temple area than elsewhere. Jesus was angry at the dishonest, greedy practices of the money changers and merchants, and he particularly disliked their presence on the Temple grounds. They were making a mockery of God's house of worship.

2:14ff John records this first clearing, or cleansing, of the Temple. A second clearing occurred at the end of Jesus' ministry, about three years later, and that event is recorded in Matthew 21:12-17; Mark 11:12-19; Luke 19:45-48.

2:16
Luke 2:49

them all out of the Temple. He drove out the sheep and oxen, scattered the money changers' coins over the floor, and turned over their tables. ¹⁶Then, going over to the people who sold doves, he told them, "Get these things out of here. Don't turn my Father's house into a marketplace!"

2:17
†Ps 69:9

¹⁷Then his disciples remembered this prophecy from the Scriptures: "Passion for God's house burns within me."*

¹⁸"What right do you have to do these things?" the Jewish leaders demanded. "If you have this authority from God, show us a miraculous sign to prove it."

2:19
Matt 26:61; 27:40
Mark 14:58
Acts 6:14

¹⁹"All right," Jesus replied. "Destroy this temple, and in three days I will raise it up."

2:17 Or *"Concern for God's house will be my undoing."* Ps 69:9.

NICODEMUS

God specializes in finding and changing people we consider out of reach. It took a while for Nicodemus to come out of the dark, but God was patient with this "undercover" believer.

Afraid of being discovered, Nicodemus made an appointment to see Jesus at night. Daylight conversations between Pharisees and Jesus tended to be antagonistic, but Nicodemus really wanted to learn. He probably got a lot more than he expected—a challenge to a new life! We know very little about Nicodemus, but we know that he left that evening's encounter a changed man. He came away with a whole new understanding of both God and himself.

Nicodemus next appears as part of the Jewish high council (7:50). As the group discussed ways to eliminate Jesus, Nicodemus raised the question of justice. Although his objection was overruled, he had spoken up. He had begun to change.

Our last picture of Nicodemus shows him joining Joseph of Arimathea in asking for Jesus' body in order to provide for its burial (19:39). Realizing what he was risking, Nicodemus was making a bold move. He was continuing to grow.

God looks for steady growth, not instant perfection. How well does your present level of spiritual growth match up with how long you have known Jesus?

Strengths and accomplishments	• One of the few religious leaders who believed in Jesus • A member of the powerful Jewish high council • A Pharisee who was attracted by Jesus' character and miracles • Joined with Joseph of Arimathea in burying Jesus
Weakness and mistake	• Limited by his fear of being publicly exposed as Jesus' follower
Lessons from his life	• Unless we are born again, we can never be part of the Kingdom of God • God is able to change those we might consider unreachable • God is patient, but persistent • If we are available, God can use us
Vital statistics	• Where: Jerusalem • Occupation: Religious leader • Contemporaries: Jesus, Annas, Caiaphas, Pilate, Joseph of Arimathea
Key verse	" 'What do you mean?' exclaimed Nicodemus. 'How can an old man go back into his mother's womb and be born again?' " (John 3:4).

Nicodemus's story is told in John 3:1–21; 7:50–52; and 19:39, 40.

2:14-16 God's Temple was being misused by people who had turned it into a marketplace. They had forgotten, or didn't care, that God's house is a place of worship, not a place for making a profit. Our attitude toward the church is wrong if we see it as a place for personal contacts or business advantage. Make sure you attend church to worship God.

2:15, 16 Jesus was obviously angry at the merchants who exploited those who had come to God's house to worship. There is a difference between uncontrolled rage and righteous indignation—yet both are called anger. We must be very careful how we use the powerful emotion of anger. It is right to be angry about injustice and sin; it is wrong to be angry over trivial personal offenses.

2:15, 16 Jesus made a whip and chased out the money changers. Does his example permit us to use violence against wrongdoers? Certain authority is granted to some, but not to all. For example, the authority to use weapons and restrain people is granted to police officers, but not to the general public. The

authority to imprison people is granted to judges, but not to individual citizens. Jesus had God's authority, something we cannot have. While we want to live like Christ, we should never try to claim his authority where it has not been given to us.

2:17 Jesus took the evil acts in the Temple as an insult against God, and thus, he did not deal with them halfheartedly. He was consumed with righteous anger against such flagrant disrespect for God.

2:19, 20 The Jews understood Jesus to mean the Temple out of which he had just driven the merchants and money changers. This was the Temple Zerubbabel had built over 500 years earlier, but Herod the Great had begun remodeling it, making it much larger and far more beautiful. It had been 46 years since this remodeling had started (20 B.C.), and it still wasn't completely finished. They understood Jesus' words to mean that this imposing building could be torn down and rebuilt in three days, and they were startled.

20"What!" they exclaimed. "It took forty-six years to build this Temple, and you can do it in three days?" 21 But by "this temple," Jesus meant his body. 22 After he was raised from the dead, the disciples remembered that he had said this. And they believed both Jesus and the Scriptures.

23 Because of the miraculous signs he did in Jerusalem at the Passover celebration, many people were convinced that he was indeed the Messiah. 24 But Jesus didn't trust them, because he knew what people were really like. 25 No one needed to tell him about human nature.

2:21
John 10:38; 14:2, 10; 17:21
1 Cor 3:16; 6:19

2:22
Luke 24:6-8
John 12:16; 14:26

2:23
John 7:31; 11:47-48

Nicodemus Visits Jesus at Night (24)

3 After dark one evening, a Jewish religious leader named Nicodemus, a Pharisee, 2 came to speak with Jesus. "Teacher," he said, "we all know that God has sent you to teach us. Your miraculous signs are proof enough that God is with you."

3 Jesus replied, "I assure you, unless you are born again,* you can never see the Kingdom of God."

4 "What do you mean?" exclaimed Nicodemus. "How can an old man go back into his mother's womb and be born again?"

5 Jesus replied, "The truth is, no one can enter the Kingdom of God without being born of water and the Spirit.* 6 Humans can reproduce only human life, but the Holy Spirit gives new life from heaven. 7 So don't be surprised at my statement that you* must be

3:1-2
John 7:50; 19:39

3:2
Matt 22:16
Acts 2:22; 10:38

3:3
John 1:13

3:5
Ezek 36:26-27
Titus 3:5
2 Pet 1:11

3:6
John 1:13
Rom 8:15-16
1 Cor 15:50
Gal 4:6

3:3 Or *born from above;* also in 3:7.   **3:5** Or *spirit.* The Greek word for *Spirit* can also be translated *wind;* see 3:8.
3:7 The Greek word for *you* is plural; also in 3:12.

2:21, 22 Jesus was not talking about the Temple made of stones, but about his body. His listeners didn't realize it, but Jesus was greater than the Temple (Matthew 12:6). His words would take on meaning for his disciples after his resurrection. That Christ so perfectly fulfilled this prediction became the strongest proof for his claims to be God.

2:23-25 The Son of God knows all about human nature. Jesus was well aware of the truth of Jeremiah 17:9, which states, "The human heart is most deceitful and desperately wicked. Who really knows how bad it is?" Jesus was discerning, and he knew that the faith of some followers was superficial. Some of the same people claiming to believe in Jesus at this time would later yell "Crucify him!" It's easy to believe when it is exciting and everyone else believes the same way. But keep your faith firm even when it isn't popular to follow Christ.

3:1 Nicodemus was a Pharisee and a member of the ruling council (called the high council, or the Sanhedrin). The Pharisees were a group of religious leaders whom Jesus and John the Baptist often criticized for being hypocrites (see the note on Matthew 3:7 for more on the Pharisees). Most Pharisees were intensely jealous of Jesus because he undermined their authority and challenged their views. But Nicodemus was searching, and he believed that Jesus had some answers. A learned teacher himself, he came to Jesus to be taught. No matter how intelligent and well educated you are, you must come to Jesus with an open mind and heart so he can teach you the truth about God.

3:1ff Nicodemus came to Jesus personally, although he could have sent one of his assistants. He wanted to examine Jesus for himself to separate fact from rumor. Perhaps Nicodemus was afraid of what his peers, the Pharisees, would say about his visit, so he came after dark. Later, when he understood that Jesus was truly the Messiah, he spoke up boldly in his defense (7:50, 51). Like Nicodemus, we must examine Jesus for ourselves—others cannot do it for us. Then, if we believe he is who he says, we will want to speak up for him.

3:3 What did Nicodemus know about the Kingdom? From the Bible he knew it would be ruled by God, it would be restored on

earth, and it would incorporate God's people. Jesus revealed to this devout Pharisee that the Kingdom would come to the whole world (3:16), not just the Jews, and that Nicodemus wouldn't be a part of it unless he was personally born again (3:5). This was a revolutionary concept: The Kingdom is personal, not national or ethnic, and its entrance requirements are repentance and spiritual rebirth. Jesus later taught that God's Kingdom has *already begun* in the hearts of believers (Luke 17:21). It will be fully realized when Jesus returns again to judge the world and abolish evil forever (Revelation 21–22).

3:5, 6 "Of water and the Spirit" could refer to (1) the contrast between physical birth (water) and spiritual birth (Spirit), or (2) being regenerated by the Spirit and signifying that rebirth by Christian baptism. The water may also represent the cleansing action of God's Holy Spirit (Titus 3:5). Nicodemus undoubtedly would have been familiar with God's promise in Ezekiel 36:25, 26. Jesus was explaining the importance of a spiritual rebirth, saying that people don't enter the Kingdom by living a better life, but by being spiritually reborn.

THE VISIT IN SAMARIA
Jesus went to Jerusalem for the Passover, cleared the Temple, and talked with Nicodemus, a religious leader, about eternal life. He then left Jerusalem and traveled in Judea. On his way to Galilee, he visited Sychar and other villages in Samaria. Unlike most Jews of the day, he did not try to avoid the region of Samaria.

3:8
Eccl 11:5

born again. 8 Just as you can hear the wind but can't tell where it comes from or where it is going, so you can't explain how people are born of the Spirit."

9 "What do you mean?" Nicodemus asked.

10 Jesus replied, "You are a respected Jewish teacher, and yet you don't understand these things? 11 I assure you, I am telling you what we know and have seen, and yet you

3:13
John 6:38, 42
Eph 4:8-10

won't believe us. 12 But if you don't even believe me when I tell you about things that happen here on earth, how can you possibly believe if I tell you what is going on in

3:14
Num 21:8-9
John 8:28; 12:34

heaven? 13 For only I, the Son of Man,* have come to earth and will return to heaven again. 14 And as Moses lifted up the bronze snake on a pole in the wilderness, so I, the Son of Man, must be lifted up on a pole,* 15 so that everyone who believes in me will

3:15
John 20:31
1 Jn 5:11, 12

have eternal life.

3:16
Rom 5:8; 8:32
1 Jn 4:9-10; 5:13

16 "For God so loved the world that he gave his only Son, so that everyone who believes in him will not perish but have eternal life. 17 God did not send his Son into the

3:17
John 12:47

world to condemn it, but to save it.

3:18
John 5:24

18 "There is no judgment awaiting those who trust him. But those who do not trust him have already been judged for not believing in the only Son of God. 19 Their judgment is

3:19
John 1:5, 9; 8:12;
9:5; 12:46

based on this fact: The light from heaven came into the world, but they loved the darkness more than the light, for their actions were evil. 20 They hate the light because

3:20
Eph 5:11-13

they want to sin in the darkness. They stay away from the light for fear their sins will be exposed and they will be punished. 21 But those who do what is right come to the light

3:21
1 Jn 1:6

gladly, so everyone can see that they are doing what God wants."

3:13 Some manuscripts add *who lives in heaven.* **3:14** Greek *must be lifted up.*

3:6 Who is the Holy Spirit? God is three persons in one—the Father, the Son, and the Holy Spirit. God became a man in Jesus so that Jesus could die for our sins. Jesus rose from the dead to offer salvation to all people through spiritual renewal and rebirth. When Jesus ascended into heaven, his physical presence left the earth, but he promised to send the Holy Spirit so that his spiritual presence would still be among humankind (see Luke 24:49). The Holy Spirit first became available to all believers at Pentecost (Acts 2). Whereas in Old Testament days the Holy Spirit empowered specific individuals for specific purposes, now all believers have the power of the Holy Spirit available to them. For more on the Holy Spirit, read 14:16-28; Romans 8:9; 1 Corinthians 12:13; and 2 Corinthians 1:22.

3:8 Jesus explained that we cannot control the work of the Holy Spirit. He works in ways we cannot predict or understand. Just as you did not control your physical birth, so you cannot control your spiritual birth. It is a gift from God through the Holy Spirit (Romans 8:16; 1 Corinthians 2:10-12; 1 Thessalonians 1:5, 6).

3:10, 11 This Jewish teacher of the Bible knew the Old Testament thoroughly, but he didn't understand what it said about the Messiah. Knowledge is not salvation. You should know the Bible, but even more important, you should understand the God whom the Bible reveals and the salvation that God offers.

3:14, 15 When the Israelites were wandering in the wilderness, God sent a plague of snakes to punish the people for their rebellious attitudes. Those doomed to die from snakebite could be healed by obeying God's command to look up at the elevated bronze snake and by believing that God would heal them if they did (see Numbers 21:8, 9). Similarly, our salvation happens when we look up to Jesus, believing he will save us. God has provided this way for us to be healed of sin's deadly bite.

3:16 The message of the Good News comes to a focus in this verse. God's love is not static or self-centered; it reaches out and draws others in. Here God sets the pattern of true love, the basis for all love relationships—when you love someone dearly, you are willing to give freely to the point of self-sacrifice. God paid dearly with the life of his Son, the highest price he could pay. Jesus accepted our punishment, paid the price for our sins, and then offered us the new life that he had bought for us. When we share the Good News with others, our love must be like Jesus'—

willingly giving up our own comfort and security so that others might join us in receiving God's love.

3:16 Some people are repulsed by the idea of eternal life because their lives are miserable. But eternal life is not an extension of a person's miserable, mortal life; eternal life is God's life embodied in Christ given to all believers now as a guarantee that they will live forever. In eternal life there is no death, sickness, enemy, evil, or sin. When we don't know Christ, we make choices as though this life is all we have. In reality, this life is just the introduction to eternity. Receive this new life by faith and begin to evaluate all that happens from an eternal perspective.

3:16 To "believe" is more than intellectual agreement that Jesus is God. It means to put our trust and confidence in him that he alone can save us. It is to put Christ in charge of our present plans and eternal destiny. Believing is both trusting his words as reliable, and relying on him for the power to change. If you have never trusted Christ, let this promise of everlasting life be yours—and believe.

3:18 People often try to protect themselves from their fears by putting their faith in something they do or have: good deeds, skill or intelligence, money or possessions. But only God can save us from the one thing that we really need to fear—eternal condemnation. We believe in God by recognizing the insufficiency of our own efforts to find salvation and by asking him to do his work in us. When Jesus talks about unbelievers, he means those who reject or ignore him completely, not those who have momentary doubts.

3:19-21 Many people don't want their lives exposed to God's light because they are afraid of what will be revealed. They don't want to be changed. Don't be surprised when these same people are threatened by your desire to obey God and do what is right, because they are afraid that the light in you may expose some of the darkness in their lives. Rather than giving in to discouragement, keep praying that they will come to see how much better it is to live in light than in darkness.

John the Baptist Tells More about Jesus (**25**)

²²Afterward Jesus and his disciples left Jerusalem, but they stayed in Judea for a while and baptized there.

     ²³At this time John the Baptist was baptizing at Aenon, near Salim, because there was plenty of water there and people kept coming to him for baptism. ²⁴This was before John was put into prison. ²⁵At that time a certain Jew began an argument with John's disciples over ceremonial cleansing. ²⁶John's disciples came to him and said, "Teacher, the man you met on the other side of the Jordan River, the one you said was the Messiah, is also baptizing people. And everybody is going over there instead of coming here to us."

     ²⁷John replied, "God in heaven appoints each person's work. ²⁸You yourselves know how plainly I told you that I am not the Messiah. I am here to prepare the way for him—that is all. ²⁹The bride will go where the bridegroom is. A bridegroom's friend rejoices with him. I am the bridegroom's friend, and I am filled with joy at his success. ³⁰He must become greater and greater, and I must become less and less.

     ³¹"He has come from above and is greater than anyone else. I am of the earth, and my understanding is limited to the things of earth, but he has come from heaven.* ³²He tells what he has seen and heard, but how few believe what he tells them! ³³Those who believe him discover that God is true. ³⁴For he is sent by God. He speaks God's words, for God's Spirit is upon him without measure or limit. ³⁵The Father loves his Son, and he has given him authority over everything. ³⁶And all who believe in God's Son have eternal life. Those who don't obey the Son will never experience eternal life, but the wrath of God remains upon them."

Jesus Talks to a Woman at the Well (**27**)

4 Jesus* learned that the Pharisees had heard, "Jesus is baptizing and making more disciples than John" ²(though Jesus himself didn't baptize them—his disciples did). ³So he left Judea to return to Galilee.

3:31 Some manuscripts omit *but he has come from heaven.*   **4:1** Some manuscripts read *The Lord.*

3:22
John 3:26; 4:1-2

3:24
Matt 4:12

3:26
John 1:7, 34

3:27
1 Cor 4:7
Heb 5:4

3:28
Mal 3:1

3:29
Matt 9:15
Rev 21:9

3:31
1 Jn 4:5

3:33
1 Jn 5:10

3:34
Luke 4:18

3:35
John 5:20; 15:9

3:36
John 3:16
1 Jn 5:12-13

4:1
John 3:22, 26

3:25ff Some people look for points of disagreement so they can sow seeds of discord, discontent, and doubt. John the Baptist ended this theological argument by focusing on his devotion to Christ. It is divisive to try to force others to believe our way. Instead, let's witness about what Christ has done for us. How can anyone argue with us about that?

3:26 John the Baptist's disciples were disturbed because people were following Jesus instead of John. It is easy to grow jealous of the popularity of another person's ministry. But we must remember that our true mission is to influence people to follow Christ, not us.

3:27 Why did John the Baptist continue to baptize after Jesus came onto the scene? Why didn't he become a disciple, too? John explained that because God had given him his work, he had to continue it until God called him to do something else. John's main purpose was to point people to Christ. Even with Jesus beginning his own ministry, John could still turn people to Jesus.

3:30 John's willingness to decrease in importance shows unusual humility. Pastors and other Christian leaders can be tempted to focus more on the success of their ministries than on Christ. Beware of those who put more emphasis on their own achievements than on God's Kingdom.

3:31-35 Jesus' testimony was trustworthy because he had come from heaven and was speaking of what he had seen there. His words were the very words of God. Your whole spiritual life depends on your answer to one question: Who is Jesus Christ? If you accept Jesus as only a prophet or teacher, you have to reject his teaching, for he claimed to be God's Son, even God himself. The heartbeat of John's Gospel is the dynamic truth that Jesus Christ is God's Son, the Messiah, the Savior, who existed from the beginning and will continue to live forever. This same Jesus has invited us to accept him and live with him eternally. When we understand who Jesus is, we are compelled to believe what he said.

3:34 God's Spirit was upon Jesus without measure or limit. Thus, Jesus was the highest revelation of God to humanity (Hebrews 1:2).

3:36 Jesus says that those who believe in him *have* (not *will* have) eternal life. To receive eternal life is to join in God's life, which by nature is eternal. Thus, eternal life begins at the moment of spiritual rebirth.

3:36 John, the author of this Gospel, has been demonstrating that Jesus is the true Son of God. Jesus sets before us the greatest choice in life. We are responsible to decide today whom we will obey (Joshua 24:15), and God wants us to choose him and life (Deuteronomy 30:15-20). The wrath of God is God's final judgment and rejection of the sinner. To put off the choice is to choose not to follow Christ. Indecision is a fatal decision.

4:1-3 Already opposition was rising against Jesus, especially from the Pharisees. They resented Jesus' popularity as well as his message, which challenged much of their teachings. Because Jesus was just beginning his ministry, it wasn't yet time to confront these leaders openly; so he left Jerusalem and traveled north toward Galilee.

4:4
Matt 10:5
Luke 9:52

4:5-6
Gen 33:19; 48:22
Josh 24:32

4:7
Gen 24:17
1 Kgs 17:10

4:9
Ezra 4:1-3; 9–10
Matt 10:5
Luke 9:52-53
John 8:48
Acts 10:48

4:10
Isa 12:3; 44:3
Jer 2:13; 17:13
John 7:37-39
1 Cor 12:13
Rev 7:17; 21:6;
22:17

4:14
John 6:35; 7:38

⁴He had to go through Samaria on the way. ⁵Eventually he came to the Samaritan village of Sychar, near the parcel of ground that Jacob gave to his son Joseph. ⁶Jacob's well was there; and Jesus, tired from the long walk, sat wearily beside the well about noontime. ⁷Soon a Samaritan woman came to draw water, and Jesus said to her, "Please give me a drink." ⁸He was alone at the time because his disciples had gone into the village to buy some food.

⁹The woman was surprised, for Jews refuse to have anything to do with Samaritans. She said to Jesus, "You are a Jew, and I am a Samaritan woman. Why are you asking me for a drink?"

¹⁰Jesus replied, "If you only knew the gift God has for you and who I am, you would ask me, and I would give you living water."

¹¹"But sir, you don't have a rope or a bucket," she said, "and this is a very deep well. Where would you get this living water? ¹²And besides, are you greater than our ancestor Jacob who gave us this well? How can you offer better water than he and his sons and his cattle enjoyed?"

¹³Jesus replied, "People soon become thirsty again after drinking this water. ¹⁴But the water I give them takes away thirst altogether. It becomes a perpetual spring within them, giving them eternal life."

4:4 After the northern kingdom, with its capital at Samaria, fell to the Assyrians, many Jews were deported to Assyria, and foreigners were brought in to settle the land and help keep the peace (2 Kings 17:24). The intermarriage between those foreigners and the remaining Jews resulted in a mixed race, impure in the opinion of Jews who lived in the southern kingdom. Thus, the pure Jews hated this mixed race, called Samaritans, because they felt that their fellow Jews who had intermarried had betrayed their people and nation. The Samaritans had set up an alternate center for worship on Mount Gerizim (4:20) to parallel the Temple at Jerusalem, but it had been destroyed 150 years earlier. The Jews did everything they could to avoid traveling through Samaria. But Jesus had no reason to live by such cultural restrictions. The route through Samaria was shorter, and that was the route he took.

4:5-7 Jacob's well was on the property originally owned by Jacob (Genesis 33:18, 19). It was not a spring-fed well, but a well into which water seeped from rain and dew, collecting at the bottom. Wells were almost always located outside the city along the main road. Twice each day, morning and evening, women came to draw water. This woman came at noon, however, probably to avoid meeting people who knew her reputation. Jesus gave this woman an extraordinary message about fresh and pure water that would quench her spiritual thirst forever.

4:7-9 This woman (1) was a Samaritan, a member of the hated mixed race, (2) was known to be living in sin, and (3) was in a public place. No respectable Jewish man would talk to a woman under such circumstances. But Jesus did. The Good News is for every person, no matter what his or her race, social position, or past sins. We must be prepared to share this Good News at any time and in any place. Jesus crossed all barriers to share the Good News, and we who follow him must do no less.

4:10 What did Jesus mean by "living water"? In the Old Testament, many verses speak of thirsting after God as one thirsts for water (Psalm 42:1; Isaiah 55:1; Jeremiah 2:13; Zechariah 13:1). God is called the fountain of life (Psalm 36:9) and the fountain of living water (Jeremiah 17:13). In saying he would bring living water that could forever quench a person's thirst for God, Jesus was claiming to be the Messiah. Only the Messiah could give this gift that satisfies the soul's desire.

4:13-15 Many spiritual functions parallel physical functions. As our bodies hunger and thirst, so do our souls need *spiritual* food and water. The woman confused the two kinds of water, perhaps because no one had ever talked with her about her spiritual hunger and thirst before. We would not think of depriving our bodies of food and water when they hunger or thirst. Why then should we deprive our souls? The living Word, Jesus Christ, and the written Word, the Bible, can satisfy our hungry and thirsty souls.

JESUS RETURNS TO GALILEE Jesus stayed in Sychar for two days, then went on to Galilee. He visited Nazareth and various towns in Galilee before arriving in Cana. From there he spoke the word of healing, and a government official's son in Capernaum was healed. The Gospel of Matthew tells us Jesus then settled in Capernaum (Matthew 4:12, 13).

15 "Please, sir," the woman said, "give me some of that water! Then I'll never be thirsty again, and I won't have to come here to haul water."

16 "Go and get your husband," Jesus told her.

17 "I don't have a husband," the woman replied.

Jesus said, "You're right! You don't have a husband—18 for you have had five husbands, and you aren't even married to the man you're living with now."

19 "Sir," the woman said, "you must be a prophet. 20 So tell me, why is it that you Jews insist that Jerusalem is the only place of worship, while we Samaritans claim it is here at Mount Gerizim,* where our ancestors worshiped?"

21 Jesus replied, "Believe me, the time is coming when it will no longer matter whether you worship the Father here or in Jerusalem. 22 You Samaritans know so little about the one you worship, while we Jews know all about him, for salvation comes through the Jews. 23 But the time is coming and is already here when true worshipers will worship the Father in spirit and in truth. The Father is looking for anyone who will worship him that way. 24 For God is Spirit, so those who worship him must worship in spirit and in truth."

25 The woman said, "I know the Messiah will come—the one who is called Christ. When he comes, he will explain everything to us."

26 Then Jesus told her, "I am the Messiah!"*

Jesus Tells about the Spiritual Harvest (28)

27 Just then his disciples arrived. They were astonished to find him talking to a woman, but none of them asked him why he was doing it or what they had been discussing. 28 The woman left her water jar beside the well and went back to the village and told everyone, 29 "Come and meet a man who told me everything I ever did! Can this be the Messiah?" 30 So the people came streaming from the village to see him.

31 Meanwhile, the disciples were urging Jesus to eat. 32 "No," he said, "I have food you don't know about."

33 "Who brought it to him?" the disciples asked each other.

34 Then Jesus explained: "My nourishment comes from doing the will of God, who sent me, and from finishing his work. 35 Do you think the work of harvesting will not

4:20 Greek *on this mountain.*   4:26 Greek *"I am, the one speaking to you."*

4:15
John 6:34

4:19
Matt 21:46
John 7:40; 9:17

4:20
Deut 11:29; 12:5-14
Josh 8:33

4:21
Mal 1:11
1 Tim 2:8

4:22
2 Kgs 17:28-41
Isa 2:3
Rom 3:1-2; 9:4-5

4:23-24
2 Cor 3:17-18
Phil 3:3

4:25
Deut 18:15

4:26
Mark 14:61-62
John 9:37

4:29
Matt 9:37
John 7:26

4:34
John 5:30, 36;
6:38; 17:4

4:35
Matt 9:37
Luke 10:2

4:15 The woman mistakenly believed that if she received the water Jesus offered, she would not have to return to the well each day. She was interested in Jesus' message because she thought it could make her life easier. But if that were always the case, people would accept Christ's message for the wrong reasons. Christ did not come to take away challenges, but to change us on the inside and to empower us to deal with problems from God's perspective.

4:15 The woman did not immediately understand what Jesus was talking about. It takes time to accept something that changes the very foundations of your life. Jesus allowed the woman time to ask questions and put pieces together for herself. Sharing the Good News will not always have immediate results. When you ask people to let Jesus change their lives, give them time to weigh the matter.

4:16-20 When this woman discovered that Jesus knew all about her private life, she quickly changed the subject. Often people become uncomfortable when the conversation is too close to home, and they try to talk about something else. As we witness, we should gently guide the conversation back to Christ. His presence exposes sin and makes people squirm, but only Christ can forgive sins and give new life.

4:20-24 The woman brought up a popular theological issue—the correct place to worship. But her question was a smoke screen to keep Jesus away from her deepest need. Jesus directed the conversation to a much more important point: The *location* of worship is not nearly as important as the *attitude* of the worshipers.

4:21-24 "God is Spirit" means he is not a physical being limited to one place. He is present everywhere, and he can be worshiped anywhere, at any time. It is not where we worship that counts, but how we worship. Is your worship genuine and true? Do you have the Holy Spirit's help? How does the Holy Spirit help us worship? The Holy Spirit prays for us (Romans 8:26), teaches us the words of Christ (14:26), and tells us we are loved (Romans 5:5).

4:22 When Jesus said, "Salvation comes through the Jews," he meant that only through the Jewish Messiah would the whole world find salvation. God had promised that through the Jewish race the whole earth would be blessed (Genesis 12:3). The Old Testament prophets had called the Jews to be a light to the other nations of the world, bringing them to a knowledge of God; and they had predicted the Messiah's coming. The woman at the well may have known of these passages and was expecting the Messiah, but she didn't realize that she was talking to him!

4:34 The "food" about which Jesus was speaking was his spiritual nourishment. It includes more than Bible study, prayer, and attending church. Spiritual nourishment also comes from doing God's will and helping to bring his work of salvation to completion. We are nourished not only by what we take in, but also by what we give out for God. In 17:4, Jesus refers to completing God's work on earth.

4:35 Sometimes Christians excuse themselves from witnessing by saying that their family or friends aren't ready to believe. Jesus, however, makes it clear that around us a continual harvest waits to

begin until the summer ends four months from now? Look around you! Vast fields are ripening all around us and are ready now for the harvest. ³⁶The harvesters are paid good wages, and the fruit they harvest is people brought to eternal life. What joy awaits both the planter and the harvester alike! ³⁷You know the saying, 'One person plants and someone else harvests.' And it's true. ³⁸I sent you to harvest where you didn't plant; others had already done the work, and you will gather the harvest."

4:37
Job 31:8
Mic 6:15

Many Samaritans Believe in Jesus (**29**)
³⁹Many Samaritans from the village believed in Jesus because the woman had said, "He told me everything I ever did!" ⁴⁰When they came out to see him, they begged him to stay at their village. So he stayed for two days, ⁴¹long enough for many of them to hear his message and believe. ⁴²Then they said to the woman, "Now we believe because we have heard him ourselves, not just because of what you told us. He is indeed the Savior of the world."

4:42
Luke 2:11
1 Jn 4:14

Jesus Preaches in Galilee (**30**/Matthew 4:12-17; Mark 1:14-15; Luke 4:14-15)
⁴³At the end of the two days' stay, Jesus went on into Galilee. ⁴⁴He had previously said, "A prophet is honored everywhere except in his own country." ⁴⁵The Galileans welcomed him, for they had been in Jerusalem at the Passover celebration and had seen all his miraculous signs.

4:43-54
//Matt 8:5-13
//Luke 7:1-10

4:44
Matt 13:57
Luke 4:24

Jesus Heals a Government Official's Son (**31**)
⁴⁶In the course of his journey through Galilee, he arrived at the town of Cana, where he had turned the water into wine. There was a government official in the city of Capernaum whose son was very sick. ⁴⁷When he heard that Jesus had come from Judea and was traveling in Galilee, he went over to Cana. He found Jesus and begged him to come to Capernaum with him to heal his son, who was about to die.

4:46
John 2:1-11

⁴⁸Jesus asked, "Must I do miraculous signs and wonders before you people will believe in me?"

4:48
1 Cor 1:22

⁴⁹The official pleaded, "Lord, please come now before my little boy dies."

⁵⁰Then Jesus told him, "Go back home. Your son will live!" And the man believed Jesus' word and started home.

4:50
Matt 8:13
Mark 7:29

⁵¹While he was on his way, some of his servants met him with the news that his son was alive and well. ⁵²He asked them when the boy had begun to feel better, and they replied, "Yesterday afternoon at one o'clock his fever suddenly disappeared!" ⁵³Then the father realized it was the same time that Jesus had told him, "Your son will live."

4:53
Acts 11:14;
16:14-15

---

be reaped. Don't let Jesus find you making excuses. Look around. You will find people ready to hear God's Word.

4:36-38 The wages Jesus offers are the joy of working for him and seeing the harvest of believers. These wages come to planter and harvester alike because both find joy in seeing new believers come into Christ's Kingdom. The phrase "others had already done the work" (4:38) may refer to the Old Testament prophets and to John the Baptist, who paved the way for the Good News.

4:39 The Samaritan woman immediately shared her experience with others. Despite her reputation, many took her invitation and came out to meet Jesus. Perhaps there are sins in our past of which we're ashamed. But Christ changes us. As people see these changes, they become curious. Use these opportunities to introduce them to Christ.

4:46-49 This government official was probably an officer in Herod's service. He had walked 20 miles to see Jesus and addressed him as "Lord," putting himself under Jesus even though he had legal authority over Jesus.

4:48 This miracle was more than a favor to one official; it was a sign to all the people. John's Gospel was written to all humankind to urge faith in Christ. Here a government official had faith that Jesus could do what he claimed. The official believed; *then* he saw a miraculous sign.

4:50 This government official not only believed Jesus could heal; he also obeyed Jesus by returning home, thus demonstrating his faith. It isn't enough for us to say we believe that Jesus can take care of our problems. We need to act as if he can. When you pray about a need or problem, live as though you believe Jesus can do what he says.

4:51 Jesus' miracles were not mere illusions, the product of wishful thinking. Although the official's son was 20 miles away, he was healed when Jesus spoke the word. Distance was no problem because Christ has mastery over space. We can never put so much space between ourselves and Christ that he can no longer help us.

4:53 Notice how the official's faith grew. First, he believed enough to ask Jesus to help his son. Second, he believed Jesus' assurance that his son would live, and he acted on it. Third, he and his whole house believed in Jesus. Faith is a gift that grows as we use it.

And the officer and his entire household believed in Jesus. ⁵⁴This was Jesus' second miraculous sign in Galilee after coming from Judea.

4:54
John 2:11

Jesus Heals a Lame Man by a Pool (42)

5 Afterward Jesus returned to Jerusalem for one of the Jewish holy days. ²Inside the city, near the Sheep Gate, was the pool of Bethesda,* with five covered porches. ³Crowds of sick people—blind, lame, or paralyzed—lay on the porches.* ⁵One of the men lying there had been sick for thirty-eight years. ⁶When Jesus saw him and knew how long he had been ill, he asked him, "Would you like to get well?"

5:1
Lev 23:1-2
Deut 16:1
John 2:13

5:2
Neh 3:1; 12:39

⁷"I can't, sir," the sick man said, "for I have no one to help me into the pool when the water is stirred up. While I am trying to get there, someone else always gets in ahead of me."

⁸Jesus told him, "Stand up, pick up your sleeping mat, and walk!"

5:8
Matt 9:6
Mark 2:11
Luke 5:24

⁹Instantly, the man was healed! He rolled up the mat and began walking! But this miracle happened on the Sabbath day. ¹⁰So the Jewish leaders objected. They said to the man who was cured, "You can't work on the Sabbath! It's illegal to carry that sleeping mat!"

5:10
Neh 13:15-20
Jer 17:21
Matt 12:2

¹¹He replied, "The man who healed me said to me, 'Pick up your sleeping mat and walk.'"

¹²"Who said such a thing as that?" they demanded.

¹³The man didn't know, for Jesus had disappeared into the crowd. ¹⁴But afterward Jesus found him in the Temple and told him, "Now you are well; so stop sinning, or something even worse may happen to you." ¹⁵Then the man went to find the Jewish leaders and told them it was Jesus who had healed him.

5:14
John 8:11

Jesus Claims to Be the Son of God (43)

¹⁶So the Jewish leaders began harassing Jesus for breaking the Sabbath rules. ¹⁷But Jesus replied, "My Father never stops working, so why should I?" ¹⁸So the Jewish

5:18
Phil 2:6
Titus 2:13
2 Pet 1:1
1 Jn 5:21

5:2 Some manuscripts read *Beth-zatha;* other manuscripts read *Bethsaida.* **5:3** Some manuscripts add *waiting for a certain movement of the water,* ⁴*for an angel of the Lord came from time to time and stirred up the water. And the first person to step down into it afterward was healed.*

JESUS TEACHES IN JERUSALEM
Between chapters 4 and 5 of John, Jesus ministered throughout Galilee, especially in Capernaum. He had been calling certain men to follow him, but it wasn't until after this trip to Jerusalem (5:1) that he chose his 12 disciples from among them.

5:1 Three festivals (or "holy days") required all Jewish males to come to Jerusalem: (1) the Festival of Passover and Unleavened Bread, (2) the Festival of Pentecost (also called the Festival of Harvest or the Festival of Weeks), and (3) the Festival of Shelters.

5:6 After 38 years, this man's problem had become a way of life. No one had ever helped him. He had no hope of ever being healed and no desire to help himself. The man's situation looked hopeless. But no matter how trapped you feel in your infirmities, God can minister to your deepest needs. Don't let a problem or hardship cause you to lose hope. God may have special work for

you to do in spite of your condition, or even because of it. Many have ministered effectively to hurting people because they have triumphed over their own hurts.

5:10 According to the Pharisees, carrying a mat on the Sabbath was work and was therefore unlawful. It did not break an Old Testament law, but it broke the Pharisees' *interpretation* of God's command to "remember to observe the Sabbath day by keeping it holy" (Exodus 20:8). This was just one of hundreds of rules they had added to the Old Testament law.

5:10 A man who hadn't walked for 38 years had been healed, but the Pharisees were more concerned about their petty rules than the life and health of a human being. It is easy to get so caught up in our man-made structures and rules that we forget the people involved. Are your guidelines for living God-made or man-made? Are they helping people, or have they become needless stumbling blocks?

5:14 This man had been lame, or paralyzed, and suddenly he could walk. This was a great miracle. But he needed an even greater miracle—to have his sins forgiven. The man was delighted to be physically healed, but he had to turn from his sins and seek God's forgiveness to be spiritually healed. God's forgiveness is the greatest gift you will ever receive. Don't neglect his gracious offer.

5:16 The Jewish leaders saw both a mighty miracle of healing and a broken rule. They threw the miracle aside as they focused their attention on the broken rule, because the rule was more important to them than the miracle. God is prepared to work in our lives, but we can shut out his miracles by limiting our views about how he works.

5:17 If God stopped every kind of work on the Sabbath, nature would fall into chaos, and sin would overrun the world. Genesis 2:2 says that God rested on the seventh day, but this can't mean that he stopped doing good. Jesus wanted to teach that when the opportunity to do good presents itself, it should not be ignored, even on the Sabbath.

leaders tried all the more to kill him. In addition to disobeying the Sabbath rules, he had spoken of God as his Father, thereby making himself equal with God.

5:19
John 8:28; 12:49;
14:10

[19]Jesus replied, "I assure you, the Son can do nothing by himself. He does only what he sees the Father doing. Whatever the Father does, the Son also does. [20]For the Father loves the Son and tells him everything he is doing, and the Son will do far greater things than healing this man. You will be astonished at what he does. [21]He will even raise from the dead anyone he wants to, just as the Father does. [22]And the Father leaves all judgment to his Son, [23]so that everyone will honor the Son, just as they honor the Father. But if you refuse to honor the Son, then you are certainly not honoring the Father who sent him.

5:21
John 11:25

5:22
John 3:17; 5:27

5:23
1 Jn 2:23

5:24
John 3:15; 20:30-31
1 Jn 3:14; 5:13

5:25
John 4:21; 6:63, 68

5:26
John 1:4; 6:57
1 Jn 5:11-12

[24]"I assure you, those who listen to my message and believe in God who sent me have eternal life. They will never be condemned for their sins, but they have already passed from death into life.

[25]"And I assure you that the time is coming, in fact it is here, when the dead will hear my voice—the voice of the Son of God. And those who listen will live. [26]The

THE CLAIMS OF CHRIST	Jesus claimed to be:	Matthew	Mark	Luke	John
Those who read the life of Christ are faced with one unavoidable question—was Jesus God? Part of any reasonable conclusion has to include the fact that he did claim to be God. We have no other choice but to agree or disagree with his claim. Eternal life is at stake in the choice.	the fulfillment of Old Testament prophecies	5:17; 14:33; 16:16, 17; 26:31, 53–56; 27:43	14:21, 61, 62	4:16–21; 7:18–23; 18:31; 22:37; 24:44	2:22; 5:45–47; 6:45; 7:40; 10:34–36; 13:18; 15:25; 20:9
	the Son of Man	8:20; 12:8; 16:27; 19:28; 20:18, 19; 24:27, 44; 25:31; 26:2, 45, 64	8:31, 38; 9:9; 10:45; 14:41	6:22; 7:33, 34; 12:8; 17:22; 18:8, 31; 19:10; 21:36	1:51; 3:13, 14; 6:27, 53; 12:23, 34
	the Son of God	11:27; 14:33; 16:16, 17; 27:43	3:11, 12; 14:61, 62	8:28; 10:22	1:18; 3:35, 36; 5:18–26; 6:40; 10:36; 11:4; 17:1; 19:7
	the Messiah/the Christ	23:9, 10; 26:63, 64	8:29, 30	4:41; 23:1, 2; 24:25–27	4:25, 26; 10:24, 25; 11:27
	Teacher/Master	26:18			13:13, 14
	one with authority to forgive		2:1–12	7:48, 49	
	Lord		5:19		13:13, 14; 20:28, 29
	Savior			19:10	3:17; 10:9

5:17ff Jesus was identifying himself with God, his Father. There could be no doubt as to his claim to be God. Jesus does not leave us the option to believe in God while ignoring God's Son (5:23). The Pharisees also called God their Father, but they realized Jesus was claiming a unique relationship with him. In response to Jesus' claim, the Pharisees had two choices: to believe him, or to accuse him of blasphemy. They chose the second.

5:19-23 Because of his unity with God, Jesus lived as God wanted him to live. Because of our identification with Jesus, we must honor him and live as he wants us to live. The questions "What would Jesus do?" and "What would Jesus have me do?" may help us make the right choices.

5:24 "Eternal life"—living forever with God—begins when you accept Jesus Christ as Savior. At that moment, new life begins in you (2 Corinthians 5:17). It is a completed transaction. You still will face physical death, but when Christ returns again, your body will be resurrected to live forever (1 Corinthians 15).

5:25 In saying that the dead will hear his voice, Jesus was talking about the spiritually dead who hear, understand, and accept him. Those who accept Jesus, the Word, will have eternal life. Jesus was also talking about the physically dead. He raised several dead people while he was on earth, and at his second coming, "all the Christians who have died" will rise to meet him (1 Thessalonians 4:16).

5:26 God is the source and Creator of life, for there is no life apart from God, here or hereafter. The life in us is a gift from him (see Deuteronomy 30:20; Psalm 36:9). Because Jesus is eternally existent with God, the Creator, he, too, is "the life" (14:6) through whom we may live eternally (see 1 John 5:11).

Father has life in himself, and he has granted his Son to have life in himself. 27 And he has given him authority to judge all mankind because he is the Son of Man. 28 Don't be so surprised! Indeed, the time is coming when all the dead in their graves will hear the voice of God's Son, 29 and they will rise again. Those who have done good will rise to eternal life, and those who have continued in evil will rise to judgment. 30 But I do nothing without consulting the Father. I judge as I am told. And my judgment is absolutely just, because it is according to the will of God who sent me; it is not merely my own.

5:27
John 9:39
Acts 10:42; 17:31

5:29
Dan 12:2
Matt 25:46
Acts 24:15

5:30
John 5:19; 6:38

Jesus Supports His Claim (**44**)

31 "If I were to testify on my own behalf, my testimony would not be valid. 32 But someone else is also testifying about me, and I can assure you that everything he says about me is true. 33 In fact, you sent messengers to listen to John the Baptist, and he preached the truth. 34 But the best testimony about me is not from a man, though I have reminded you about John's testimony so you might be saved. 35 John shone brightly for a while, and you benefited and rejoiced. 36 But I have a greater witness than John—my teachings and my miracles. They have been assigned to me by the Father, and they testify that the Father has sent me. 37 And the Father himself has also testified about me. You have never heard his voice or seen him face to face, 38 and you do not have his message in your hearts, because you do not believe me—the one he sent to you.

5:31
John 8:13-14

5:32
John 8:18

5:36
John 10:25, 38;
14:11; 15:24
1 Jn 5:9

5:37
Deut 4:12
John 1:18; 8:18
1 Tim 1:17

5:38
1 Jn 2:14

39 "You search the Scriptures because you believe they give you eternal life. But the Scriptures point to me! 40 Yet you refuse to come to me so that I can give you this eternal life.

5:39
Luke 24:27, 44
Acts 13:27
Rom 2:17-20

41 "Your approval or disapproval means nothing to me, 42 because I know you don't have God's love within you. 43 For I have come to you representing my Father, and you refuse to welcome me, even though you readily accept others who represent only themselves. 44 No wonder you can't believe! For you gladly honor each other, but you don't care about the honor that comes from God alone.

5:41
John 12:43

5:45
John 9:28
Rom 2:17

45 "Yet it is not I who will accuse you of this before the Father. Moses will accuse you! Yes, Moses, on whom you set your hopes. 46 But if you had believed Moses, you would have believed me because he wrote about me. 47 And since you don't believe what he wrote, how will you believe what I say?"

5:46
Gen 3:15
Deut 18:15, 18
Luke 24:27, 44
Acts 26:22, 23

5:47
Luke 16:31

Jesus Feeds Five Thousand (**96**/Matthew 14:13-21; Mark 6:30-44; Luke 9:10-17)

6 After this, Jesus crossed over the Sea of Galilee, also known as the Sea of Tiberias. 2 And a huge crowd kept following him wherever he went, because they saw his miracles as he healed the sick. 3 Then Jesus went up into the hills and sat down with his

6:1-13
//Matt 14:13-21
//Mark 6:32-44
//Luke 9:10-17

5:27 The Old Testament mentioned three signs of the coming Messiah. In this chapter, John shows that Jesus has fulfilled all three signs. Authority to judge is given to him as the Son of Man (cf. 5:27 with Daniel 7:13, 14). The lame and sick are healed (cf. 5:20, 21 with Isaiah 35:6; Jeremiah 31:8, 9). The dead are raised to life (cf. 5:21, 28 with Deuteronomy 32:39; 1 Samuel 2:6; 2 Kings 5:7).

5:29 Those who have rebelled against Christ will be resurrected, too, but they will hear God's judgment against them and will be sentenced to eternity apart from him. There are those who wish to live well on earth, ignore God, and then see death as final rest. Jesus does not allow unbelieving people to see death as the end of it all. There is a judgment to face.

5:31ff Jesus claimed to be equal with God (5:18), to give eternal life (5:24), to be the source of life (5:26), and to judge sin (5:27). These statements make it clear that Jesus was claiming to be divine—an almost unbelievable claim, but one that was supported by another witness, John the Baptist.

5:39, 40 The religious leaders knew what the Bible said but failed to apply its words to their lives. They knew the teachings of the Scriptures but failed to see the Messiah to whom the Scriptures pointed. They knew the rules but missed the Savior. Entrenched in their own religious system, they refused to let the Son of God change their lives. Don't become so involved in "religion" that you miss Christ.

5:41 Whose praise do you seek? The religious leaders enjoyed great prestige in Israel, but their stamp of approval meant nothing to Jesus. He was concerned about God's approval. This is a good principle for us. If even the highest officials in the world approve of our actions and God does not, we should be concerned. But if God approves, even though others don't, we should be content.

5:45 The Pharisees prided themselves on being the true followers of their ancestor Moses. They were trying to follow every one of his laws to the letter, and they even added some of their own. Jesus' warning that Moses would accuse them stung them to fury. Moses wrote about Jesus (Genesis 3:15; Numbers 21:9; 24:17; Deuteronomy 18:15), yet the religious leaders refused to believe Jesus when he came.

6:4
John 11:55

6:5
John 1:43

6:8
John 1:40

6:9
2 Kgs 4:43
John 21:9, 13

6:14
Deut 18:15, 18
Acts 3:22; 7:37

6:16-23
//Matt 14:23-33
//Mark 6:47-51

6:19
Job 9:8

disciples around him. ⁴(It was nearly time for the annual Passover celebration.) ⁵Jesus soon saw a great crowd of people climbing the hill, looking for him. Turning to Philip, he asked, "Philip, where can we buy bread to feed all these people?" ⁶He was testing Philip, for he already knew what he was going to do.

⁷Philip replied, "It would take a small fortune* to feed them!"

⁸Then Andrew, Simon Peter's brother, spoke up. ⁹"There's a young boy here with five barley loaves and two fish. But what good is that with this huge crowd?"

¹⁰"Tell everyone to sit down," Jesus ordered. So all of them—the men alone numbered five thousand—sat down on the grassy slopes. ¹¹Then Jesus took the loaves, gave thanks to God, and passed them out to the people. Afterward he did the same with the fish. And they all ate until they were full. ¹²"Now gather the leftovers," Jesus told his disciples, "so that nothing is wasted." ¹³There were only five barley loaves to start with, but twelve baskets were filled with the pieces of bread the people did not eat!

¹⁴When the people saw this miraculous sign, they exclaimed, "Surely, he is the Prophet* we have been expecting!" ¹⁵Jesus saw that they were ready to take him by force and make him king, so he went higher into the hills alone.

Jesus Walks on Water (**97**/Matthew 14:22-33; Mark 6:45-52)

¹⁶That evening his disciples went down to the shore to wait for him. ¹⁷But as darkness fell and Jesus still hadn't come back, they got into the boat and headed out across the lake toward Capernaum. ¹⁸Soon a gale swept down upon them as they rowed, and the sea grew very rough. ¹⁹They were three or four miles* out when suddenly they saw Jesus

6:7 Greek *200 denarii.* A denarius was the equivalent of a full day's wage.   **6:14** See Deut 18:15, 18.   **6:19** Greek *25 or 30 stadia* [4.6 or 5.5 kilometers].

6:5 If anyone knew where to get food, it would have been Philip because he was from Bethsaida, a town about nine miles away (1:44). Jesus was testing Philip to strengthen his faith. By asking for a human solution (knowing that there was none), Jesus highlighted the powerful and miraculous act that he was about to perform.

6:5-7 When Jesus asked Philip where they could buy a great amount of bread, Philip started assessing the probable cost. Jesus wanted to teach him that financial resources are not the most important ones. We can limit what God does in us by assuming what is and is not possible. Is there some impossible task that you believe God wants you to do? Don't let your estimate of what can't be done keep you from taking on the task. God can do the miraculous; trust him to provide the resources.

6:8, 9 The disciples are contrasted with the youngster who brought what he had. They certainly had more resources than the boy, but they knew they didn't have enough, so they didn't give anything at all. The boy gave what little he had, and it made all the difference. If we offer nothing to God, he will have nothing to use. But he can take what little we have and turn it into something great.

6:8, 9 In performing his miracles, Jesus usually preferred to work through people. Here he took what a young child offered and used it to accomplish one of the most spectacular miracles recorded in the Gospels. Age is no barrier to Christ. Never think you are too young or old to be of service to him.

6:13 There is a lesson in the leftovers. God gives in abundance. He takes whatever we can offer him in time, ability, or resources and multiplies its effectiveness beyond our wildest expectations. If you take the first step in making yourself available to God, he will show you how greatly you can be used to advance the work of his Kingdom.

6:14 "The Prophet" is the one prophesied by Moses (Deuteronomy 18:15).

6:18 The Sea of Galilee is 650 feet below sea level, 150 feet deep, and surrounded by hills. These physical features make it subject to sudden windstorms that would cause extremely high waves. Such storms were expected on this lake, but they were nevertheless frightening. When Jesus came to the disciples during a storm, walking on the water (three and a half miles from shore), he told them not to be afraid. We often face spiritual and emotional storms and feel tossed about like a small boat on a big lake. In spite of terrifying circumstances, if we trust our lives to Christ for his safekeeping, he will give us peace in any storm.

6:18, 19 The disciples, terrified, probably thought they were seeing a ghost (Mark 6:49). But if they had thought about all they had already seen Jesus do, they could have accepted this miracle. They were frightened—they didn't expect Jesus to come, and they weren't prepared for his help. Faith is a mind-set that *expects* God to act. When we act on this expectation, we can overcome our fears.

JESUS WALKS ON THE WATER
Jesus fed the 5,000 on a hill near the Sea of Galilee at Bethsaida. The disciples set out across the sea toward Capernaum. But they encountered a storm—and Jesus came walking to them on the water! The boat landed at Gennesaret (Mark 6:53); from there they went back to Capernaum.

walking on the water toward the boat. They were terrified, ²⁰but he called out to them, "I am here! Don't be afraid." ²¹Then they were eager to let him in, and immediately the boat arrived at their destination!

6:20
Matt 14:27

Jesus Is the True Bread from Heaven (99)

²²The next morning, back across the lake, crowds began gathering on the shore, waiting to see Jesus. For they knew that he and his disciples had come over together and that the disciples had gone off in their boat, leaving him behind. ²³Several boats from Tiberias landed near the place where the Lord had blessed the bread and the people had eaten. ²⁴When the crowd saw that Jesus wasn't there, nor his disciples, they got into the boats and went across to Capernaum to look for him. ²⁵When they arrived and found him, they asked, "Teacher, how did you get here?"

6:23
John 6:11

²⁶Jesus replied, "The truth is, you want to be with me because I fed you, not because you saw the miraculous sign. ²⁷But you shouldn't be so concerned about perishable things like food. Spend your energy seeking the eternal life that I, the Son of Man, can give you. For God the Father has sent me for that very purpose."

6:27
Matt 3:17; 17:5
Mark 1:11; 9:7
Luke 3:22
John 1:33; 4:14;
6:50-51, 54, 58
Acts 2:22
Rom 6:23

²⁸They replied, "What does God want us to do?"

²⁹Jesus told them, "This is what God wants you to do: Believe in the one he has sent."

6:29
1 Jn 3:23

³⁰They replied, "You must show us a miraculous sign if you want us to believe in you. What will you do for us? ³¹After all, our ancestors ate manna while they journeyed through the wilderness! As the Scriptures say, 'Moses gave them bread from heaven.'*"

6:31
Exod 16:15
Num 11:7-9
Neh 9:15
†Pss 78:24; 105:40

³²Jesus said, "I assure you, Moses didn't give them bread from heaven. My Father did. And now he offers you the true bread from heaven. ³³The true bread of God is the one who comes down from heaven and gives life to the world."

6:33
John 6:41, 50

³⁴"Sir," they said, "give us that bread every day of our lives."

6:35
John 4:14; 6:48;
7:37-38

³⁵Jesus replied, "I am the bread of life. No one who comes to me will ever be hungry again. Those who believe in me will never thirst. ³⁶But you haven't believed in me even though you have seen me. ³⁷However, those the Father has given me will come to me, and I will never reject them. ³⁸For I have come down from heaven to do the will of God who sent me, not to do what I want. ³⁹And this is the will of God, that I should not lose even one of all those he has given me, but that I should raise them to eternal life at the last day. ⁴⁰For it is my Father's will that all who see his Son and believe in him should have eternal life—that I should raise them at the last day."

6:37
John 10:28-29;
17:2, 24

6:38
John 4:34; 5:30

6:39
John 10:28-29;
17:12; 18:9

6:40
John 12:45

6:31 Exod 16:4; Ps 78:24.

6:26 Jesus criticized the people who followed him only for the physical and temporal benefits and not for the satisfying of their spiritual hunger. Many people use religion to gain prestige, comfort, or even political votes. But those are self-centered motives. True believers follow Jesus simply because they know he has the truth and his way is the way to live.

6:28, 29 Many sincere seekers for God are puzzled about what he wants them to do. The religions of the world are humankind's attempts to answer this question. But Jesus' reply is brief and simple: We must believe on him whom God has sent. Satisfying God does not come from the work we *do*, but from whom we *believe*. The first step is accepting that Jesus is who he claims to be. All spiritual development is built on this affirmation. Declare to Jesus, "You are the Messiah, the Son of the living God" (Matthew 16:16), and embark on a life of belief that is satisfying to your Creator.

6:35 People eat bread to satisfy physical hunger and to sustain physical life. We can satisfy spiritual hunger and sustain spiritual life only by a right relationship with Jesus Christ. No wonder he called himself the bread of life. But bread must be eaten to sustain life, and Christ must be invited into our daily walk to sustain spiritual life.

6:37, 38 Jesus did not work independently of God the Father, but in union with him. This should give us even more assurance of being welcomed into God's presence and being protected by him. Jesus' purpose was to do the will of God, not to satisfy Jesus' human desires. When we follow Jesus, we should have the same purpose.

6:39 Jesus said he would not lose even one person whom the Father had given him. Thus, anyone who makes a sincere commitment to believe in Jesus Christ as Savior is secure in God's promise of eternal life. Christ will not let his people be overcome by Satan and lose their salvation (see also 17:12; Philippians 1:6).

6:40 Those who put their faith in Christ will be resurrected from physical death to eternal life with God when Christ comes again (see 1 Corinthians 15:52; 1 Thessalonians 4:16).

The People Disagree That Jesus Is from Heaven (**100**)

6:41
John 6:33, 35, 51

6:42
Luke 4:22
John 7:27-28

6:44
Jer 31:3
John 6:65; 12:32

6:45
†Isa 54:13
Jer 31:33-34
1 Thes 4:9
Heb 8:10, 11

6:46
John 1:18; 5:37

6:47
John 3:15, 16, 36

6:48
John 6:35, 41, 51, 58

6:51
John 10:10-11
Heb 10:10

6:54
John 6:39-40, 44

6:56
John 14:20; 15:4-7; 17:21-23
1 Jn 2:24; 3:24

6:57
John 5:26

6:58
John 6:31

6:62
Acts 1:9-11
Eph 4:8

6:63
Rom 8:2
1 Cor 15:45
1 Pet 3:18

⁴¹Then the people* began to murmur in disagreement because he had said, "I am the bread from heaven." ⁴²They said, "This is Jesus, the son of Joseph. We know his father and mother. How can he say, 'I came down from heaven'?"

⁴³But Jesus replied, "Don't complain about what I said. ⁴⁴For people can't come to me unless the Father who sent me draws them to me, and at the last day I will raise them from the dead. ⁴⁵As it is written in the Scriptures, 'They will all be taught by God.'* Everyone who hears and learns from the Father comes to me. ⁴⁶(Not that anyone has ever seen the Father; only I, who was sent from God, have seen him.)

⁴⁷"I assure you, anyone who believes in me already has eternal life. ⁴⁸Yes, I am the bread of life! ⁴⁹Your ancestors ate manna in the wilderness, but they all died. ⁵⁰However, the bread from heaven gives eternal life to everyone who eats it. ⁵¹I am the living bread that came down out of heaven. Anyone who eats this bread will live forever; this bread is my flesh, offered so the world may live."

⁵²Then the people began arguing with each other about what he meant. "How can this man give us his flesh to eat?" they asked.

⁵³So Jesus said again, "I assure you, unless you eat the flesh of the Son of Man and drink his blood, you cannot have eternal life within you. ⁵⁴But those who eat my flesh and drink my blood have eternal life, and I will raise them at the last day. ⁵⁵For my flesh is the true food, and my blood is the true drink. ⁵⁶All who eat my flesh and drink my blood remain in me, and I in them. ⁵⁷I live by the power of the living Father who sent me; in the same way, those who partake of me will live because of me. ⁵⁸I am the true bread from heaven. Anyone who eats this bread will live forever and not die as your ancestors did, even though they ate the manna."

⁵⁹He said these things while he was teaching in the synagogue in Capernaum.

Many Disciples Desert Jesus (**101**)

⁶⁰Even his disciples said, "This is very hard to understand. How can anyone accept it?"

⁶¹Jesus knew within himself that his disciples were complaining, so he said to them, "Does this offend you? ⁶²Then what will you think if you see me, the Son of Man, return to heaven again? ⁶³It is the Spirit who gives eternal life. Human effort accomplishes

6:41 Greek *Jewish people;* also in 6:52.   **6:45** Isa 54:13.

6:41 The religious leaders grumbled because they could not accept Jesus' claim of divinity. They saw him only as a carpenter from Nazareth. They refused to believe that Jesus was God's divine Son, and they could not tolerate his message. Many people reject Christ because they say they cannot believe he is the Son of God. In reality, the demands that Christ makes for their loyalty and obedience are what they can't accept. So to protect themselves from the message, they reject the messenger.

6:44 God, not people, plays the most active role in salvation. When someone chooses to believe in Jesus Christ as Savior, he or she does so only in response to the urging of God's Holy Spirit. God does the urging; then we decide whether or not to believe. Thus, no one can believe in Jesus without God's help.

6:45 Jesus was alluding to an Old Testament view of the messianic Kingdom in which all people are taught directly by God (Isaiah 54:13; Jeremiah 31:31-34). He was stressing the importance of not merely hearing, but learning. We are taught by God through the Bible, our experiences, the thoughts the Holy Spirit brings, and relationships with other Christians. Are you open to God's teaching?

6:47 As used here, *believes* means "continues to believe." We do not believe merely once; we keep on believing in and trusting Jesus.

6:47ff The religious leaders frequently asked Jesus to prove to them why he was better than the prophets they already had. Jesus here referred to the manna that Moses had given their ancestors in the wilderness (see Exodus 16). This bread was physical and temporal. The people ate it, and it sustained them

for a day. But they had to get more bread every day, and this bread could not keep them from dying. Jesus, who is much greater than Moses, offers himself as the spiritual bread from heaven that satisfies completely and leads to eternal life.

6:51 How can Jesus give us his flesh as bread to eat? To eat living bread means to accept Christ into our lives and become united with him. We are united with Christ in two ways: (1) by believing in his death (the sacrifice of his flesh) and resurrection and (2) by devoting ourselves to living as he requires, depending on his teaching for guidance and trusting in the Holy Spirit for power.

6:56 This was a shocking message—to eat flesh and drink blood sounded cannibalistic. The idea of drinking any blood, let alone human blood, was repugnant to the religious leaders because the law forbade it (Leviticus 17:10, 11). Jesus was not talking about literal blood, of course. He was saying that his life had to become their own, but they could not accept this concept. The apostle Paul later used the body and blood imagery in talking about Communion (see 1 Corinthians 11:23-26).

6:63, 65 The Holy Spirit gives spiritual life; without the work of the Holy Spirit, we cannot even see our need for new life (14:17). All spiritual renewal begins and ends with God. He reveals truth to us, lives within us, and then enables us to respond to that truth.

nothing. And the very words I have spoken to you are spirit and life. 64But some of you don't believe me." (For Jesus knew from the beginning who didn't believe, and he knew who would betray him.) 65Then he said, "That is what I meant when I said that people can't come to me unless the Father brings them to me."

66At this point many of his disciples turned away and deserted him. 67Then Jesus turned to the Twelve and asked, "Are you going to leave, too?"

68Simon Peter replied, "Lord, to whom would we go? You alone have the words that give eternal life. 69We believe them, and we know you are the Holy One of God."

70Then Jesus said, "I chose the twelve of you, but one is a devil." 71He was speaking of Judas, son of Simon Iscariot, one of the Twelve, who would betray him.

6:64
John 13:11

6:65
John 6:44

6:68
John 6:63

6:69
Matt 16:16
Mark 1:24; 8:29
Luke 9:20
1 Jn 2:20

2. Jesus encounters conflict with the religious leaders

Jesus' Brothers Ridicule Him (**121**)

7 After this, Jesus stayed in Galilee, going from village to village. He wanted to stay out of Judea where the Jewish leaders were plotting his death. 2But soon it was time for the Festival of Shelters, 3and Jesus' brothers urged him to go to Judea for the celebration. "Go where your followers can see your miracles!" they scoffed. 4"You can't become a public figure if you hide like this! If you can do such wonderful things, prove it to the world!" 5For even his brothers didn't believe in him.

6Jesus replied, "Now is not the right time for me to go. But you can go anytime, and it will make no difference. 7The world can't hate you, but it does hate me because I accuse it of sin and evil. 8You go on. I am not yet* ready to go to this festival, because my time has not yet come." 9So Jesus remained in Galilee.

7:1
John 5:18; 7:19;
8:37, 40

7:2
Lev 23:34
Deut 16:16

7:3
Matt 12:46

7:6
John 2:4; 7:30; 8:20

7:7
John 15:18

Jesus Teaches Openly at the Temple (**123**)

10But after his brothers had left for the festival, Jesus also went, though secretly, staying out of public view. 11The Jewish leaders tried to find him at the festival and

7:11
John 11:56

7:8 Some manuscripts omit *yet.*

6:66 Why did Jesus' words cause many of his followers to desert him? (1) They may have realized that he wasn't going to be the conquering Messiah-King they expected. (2) He refused to give in to their self-centered requests. (3) He emphasized faith, not deeds. (4) His teachings were difficult to understand, and some of his words were offensive. As we grow in our faith, we may be tempted to turn away because Jesus' lessons are difficult. Will your response be to give up, ignore certain teachings, or reject Christ? Instead, ask God to show you what the teachings mean and how they apply to your life. Then have the courage to act on God's truth.

6:67 There is no middle ground with Jesus. When he asked the disciples if they would also leave, he was showing that they could either accept or reject him. Jesus was not trying to repel people with his teachings. He was simply telling the truth. The more the people heard Jesus' real message, the more they divided into two camps—the honest seekers who wanted to understand more, and those who rejected Jesus because they didn't like what they had heard.

6:67, 68 After many of Jesus' followers had deserted him, he asked the 12 disciples if they were also going to leave. Peter replied, "To whom would we go?" In his straightforward way, Peter answered for all of us—there is no other way. Though there are many philosophies and self-styled authorities, Jesus alone has the words of eternal life. People look everywhere for eternal life and miss Christ, the only source. Stay with him, especially when you are confused or feel alone.

6:70 In response to Jesus' message, some people left; others stayed and truly believed; and some, like Judas, stayed but tried to use Jesus for personal gain. Many people today turn away from Christ. Others pretend to follow, going to church for status,

approval of family and friends, or business contacts. But there are only two real responses to Jesus—you either accept him or reject him. How have you responded to Christ?

6:71 For more information on Judas, see his Profile in Mark 14.

7:2 The Festival of Shelters is described in Leviticus 23:33ff. This event occurred in October, about six months after the Passover celebration mentioned in John 6:2-5. The festival commemorated the days when the Israelites wandered in the wilderness and lived in shelters (Leviticus 23:43).

7:3-5 Jesus' brothers had a difficult time believing in him. Some of these brothers would eventually become leaders in the church (James, for example), but for several years they were embarrassed by Jesus. After Jesus died and rose again, they finally believed. We today have every reason to believe because we have the full record of Jesus' miracles, death, and resurrection. We also have the evidence of what the Good News has done in people's lives through the centuries. Don't miss this opportunity to believe in God's Son.

7:7 Because the world hated Jesus, we who follow him can expect that many people will hate us as well. If circumstances are going too well, ask if you are following Christ as you should. We can be grateful when life goes well, but we must make sure it is not at the cost of following Jesus halfheartedly or not at all.

7:10 Jesus came with the greatest gift ever offered, so why did he often act secretly? The religious leaders hated him, and many would refuse his gift of salvation, no matter what he said or did. The more Jesus taught and worked publicly, the more these leaders would cause trouble for him and his followers. So it was necessary for Jesus to teach and work as quietly as possible. Many people today have the privilege of teaching, preaching, and worshiping publicly with little persecution. These believers should be grateful and make the most of their opportunities to proclaim the Good News.

7:12
John 7:40-43

7:13
John 9:22-23

7:15
Matt 13:54
Luke 2:47
Acts 4:13

7:16
John 8:28; 12:49;
14:10

7:18
John 5:41, 44;
8:50, 54

7:19
John 1:17; 7:1, 25;
8:37-40

7:20
John 8:48, 52;
10:20

7:21-22
Gen 17:10-13
Lev 12:3

7:23
John 5:8-10, 16
Acts 7:8

7:24
Isa 11:3-4
John 8:15

7:27
John 9:29

7:28-29
John 8:26, 55;
17:25

7:30
John 8:20

7:31
John 2:23; 8:30;
10:42; 11:45;
12:11, 42

kept asking if anyone had seen him. 12 There was a lot of discussion about him among the crowds. Some said, "He's a wonderful man," while others said, "He's nothing but a fraud, deceiving the people." 13 But no one had the courage to speak favorably about him in public, for they were afraid of getting in trouble with the Jewish leaders.

14 Then, midway through the festival, Jesus went up to the Temple and began to teach. 15 The Jewish leaders were surprised when they heard him. "How does he know so much when he hasn't studied everything we've studied?" they asked.

16 So Jesus told them, "I'm not teaching my own ideas, but those of God who sent me. 17 Anyone who wants to do the will of God will know whether my teaching is from God or is merely my own. 18 Those who present their own ideas are looking for praise for themselves, but those who seek to honor the one who sent them are good and genuine. 19 None of you obeys the law of Moses! In fact, you are trying to kill me."

20 The crowd replied, "You're demon possessed! Who's trying to kill you?"

21 Jesus replied, "I worked on the Sabbath by healing a man, and you were offended. 22 But you work on the Sabbath, too, when you obey Moses' law of circumcision. (Actually, this tradition of circumcision is older than the law of Moses; it goes back to Abraham.) 23 For if the correct time for circumcising your son falls on the Sabbath, you go ahead and do it, so as not to break the law of Moses. So why should I be condemned for making a man completely well on the Sabbath? 24 Think this through and you will see that I am right."

25 Some of the people who lived there in Jerusalem said among themselves, "Isn't this the man they are trying to kill? 26 But here he is, speaking in public, and they say nothing to him. Can it be that our leaders know that he really is the Messiah? 27 But how could he be? For we know where this man comes from. When the Messiah comes, he will simply appear; no one will know where he comes from."

28 While Jesus was teaching in the Temple, he called out, "Yes, you know me, and you know where I come from. But I represent one you don't know, and he is true. 29 I know him because I have come from him, and he sent me to you." 30 Then the leaders tried to arrest him; but no one laid a hand on him, because his time had not yet come.

31 Many among the crowds at the Temple believed in him. "After all," they said, "would you expect the Messiah to do more miraculous signs than this man has done?"

7:13 The religious leaders had a great deal of power over the common people. Apparently these leaders couldn't do much to Jesus at this time, but they threatened anyone who might publicly support him, most likely with excommunication. Excommunication from the synagogue was one of the reprisals for believing in Jesus (9:22). To a Jew, this was a severe punishment.

7:13 Everyone was talking about Jesus! But when it came time to speak up for him in public, no one said a word. All were afraid. Fear can stifle our witness. Although many people talk about Christ in church, when it comes to making a public statement about their faith, they are often embarrassed. Jesus says that he will acknowledge us before God if we acknowledge him before others (Matthew 10:32). Be courageous! Speak up for Christ!

7:16-18 Those who attempt to know God's will and do it will know intuitively that Jesus was telling the truth about himself. Have you ever listened to religious speakers and wondered if they were telling the truth? Test them: (1) Their words should agree with, not contradict, the Bible; (2) their words should point to God and his will, not themselves.

7:19 The Pharisees spent their days trying to achieve holiness by keeping the meticulous rules that they had added to God's laws. Jesus' accusation that they didn't keep Moses' laws stung them deeply. In spite of their pompous pride in themselves and their rules, they did not even fulfill a legalistic religion, for they were living far below what the law of Moses required. Murder was certainly against the law. Jesus' followers should do *more* than the moral law requires, not by adding to its requirements, but by

going beyond and beneath the mere dos and don'ts of the law to the spirit of the law.

7:20 Most of the people were probably not aware of the plot to kill Jesus (5:18). There was a small group looking for the right opportunity to kill him, but most were still trying to decide what they believed about him.

7:21-23 According to Moses' law, circumcision was to be performed eight days after a baby's birth (Genesis 17:9-14; Leviticus 12:3). This rite was carried out on all Jewish males to demonstrate their identity as part of God's covenant people. If the eighth day after birth was a Sabbath, the circumcision would still be performed (even though it was considered work). While the religious leaders allowed certain exceptions to Sabbath laws, they allowed none to Jesus, who was simply showing mercy to those who needed healing.

7:26 This chapter shows the many reactions people had toward Jesus. They called him a wonderful man (7:12), a fraud (7:12), a demon-possessed man (7:20), the Messiah (7:26), and the Prophet, whose coming had been predicted by Moses (7:40). We must make up our own minds about who Jesus is, knowing that whatever we decide will have eternal consequences.

7:27 There was a popular tradition that the Messiah would simply appear. But those who believed this tradition were ignoring the Scriptures that clearly predicted the Messiah's birthplace (Micah 5:2).

Religious Leaders Attempt to Arrest Jesus (**124**)

³²When the Pharisees heard that the crowds were murmuring such things, they and the leading priests sent Temple guards to arrest Jesus. ³³But Jesus told them, "I will be here a little longer. Then I will return to the one who sent me. ³⁴You will search for me but not find me. And you won't be able to come where I am."

³⁵The Jewish leaders were puzzled by this statement. "Where is he planning to go?" they asked. "Maybe he is thinking of leaving the country and going to the Jews in other lands, or maybe even to the Gentiles! ³⁶What does he mean when he says, 'You will search for me but not find me,' and 'You won't be able to come where I am'?"

³⁷On the last day, the climax of the festival, Jesus stood and shouted to the crowds, "If you are thirsty, come to me! ³⁸If you believe in me, come and drink! For the Scriptures declare that rivers of living water will flow out from within."* ³⁹(When he said "living water," he was speaking of the Spirit, who would be given to everyone believing in him. But the Spirit had not yet been given, because Jesus had not yet entered into his glory.)

⁴⁰When the crowds heard him say this, some of them declared, "This man surely is the Prophet."* ⁴¹Others said, "He is the Messiah." Still others said, "But he can't be! Will the Messiah come from Galilee? ⁴²For the Scriptures clearly state that the Messiah will be born of the royal line of David, in Bethlehem, the village where King David was born."* ⁴³So the crowd was divided in their opinion about him. ⁴⁴And some wanted him arrested, but no one touched him.

⁴⁵The Temple guards who had been sent to arrest him returned to the leading priests and Pharisees. "Why didn't you bring him in?" they demanded.

⁴⁶"We have never heard anyone talk like this!" the guards responded.

⁴⁷"Have you been led astray, too?" the Pharisees mocked. ⁴⁸"Is there a single one of us rulers or Pharisees who believes in him? ⁴⁹These ignorant crowds do, but what do they know about it? A curse on them anyway!"

⁵⁰Nicodemus, the leader who had met with Jesus earlier, then spoke up. ⁵¹"Is it legal to convict a man before he is given a hearing?" he asked.

7:33
John 13:33; 16:5

7:34
John 8:21; 13:33

7:37
Isa 55:1
John 4:10, 14; 6:35
Rev 22:17

7:38
Prov 18:4
Isa 58:11
Ezek 47:1-10
Joel 3:18

7:39
John 14:17-18;
16:7; 20:22
Rom 8:9
1 Cor 15:45
2 Cor 3:17

7:40
Deut 18:15
John 6:14

7:41
John 1:46

7:42
2 Sam 7:12
Mic 5:2
Matt 1:1; 2:5-10
Luke 2:4

7:44
John 7:30

7:46
Matt 7:28

7:48
John 12:42

7:50
John 3:1-2; 19:39

7:51
Deut 1:16

7:37-38 Or *"Let anyone who is thirsty come to me and drink.* ³⁸*For the Scriptures declare that rivers of living water will flow from the heart of those who believe in me."* **7:40** See Deut 18:15, 18. **7:42** See Mic 5:2.

7:38 Jesus' words, "come and drink," alluded to the theme of many Bible passages that talk about the Messiah's life-giving blessings (Isaiah 12:2, 3; 44:3, 4; 58:11). In promising to give the Holy Spirit to all who believed, Jesus was claiming to be the Messiah, for that was something only the Messiah could do.

7:38 Jesus used the term *living water* in 4:10 to indicate eternal life. Here he uses the term to refer to the Holy Spirit. The two go together: Wherever the Holy Spirit is accepted, he brings eternal life. Jesus teaches more about the Holy Spirit in chapters 14–16. The Holy Spirit empowered Jesus' followers at Pentecost (Acts 2) and has since been available to all who believe in Jesus as Savior.

7:40-44 The crowd was asking questions about Jesus. Some believed, others were hostile, and others disqualified Jesus as the Messiah because he was from Nazareth, not Bethlehem (Micah 5:2). But he *was* born in Bethlehem (Luke 2:1-7), although he grew up in Nazareth. If they had looked more carefully, they would not have jumped to the wrong conclusions. When you search for God's truth, make sure you look carefully and thoughtfully at the Bible with an open heart and mind. Don't jump to conclusions before knowing more of what the Bible says.

7:44-46 Although the Romans ruled Palestine, they gave the Jewish religious leaders authority over minor civil and religious affairs. The religious leaders supervised their own Temple guards and gave the officers power to arrest anyone causing a disturbance or breaking any of their ceremonial laws. Because these leaders had developed hundreds of trivial laws, it was almost impossible for anyone, even the leaders themselves, not

to break, neglect, or ignore at least a few of them some of the time. But these Temple guards couldn't find one reason to arrest Jesus. And as they listened to Jesus to try to find evidence, they couldn't help hearing the wonderful words he said.

7:46-49 The Jewish leaders saw themselves as an elite group that alone had the truth, and they resisted the truth about Christ because it wasn't *theirs* to begin with. It is easy to think that we have the truth and that those who disagree with us do not have any truth at all. But God's truth is available to everyone. Don't copy the Pharisees' self-centered and narrow attitude.

7:50-52 This passage offers additional insight into Nicodemus, the Pharisee who visited Jesus at night (chapter 3). Apparently Nicodemus had become a secret believer. Since most of the Pharisees hated Jesus and wanted to kill him, Nicodemus risked his reputation and high position when he spoke up for Jesus. His statement was bold, and the Pharisees immediately became suspicious. After Jesus' death, Nicodemus brought spices for his body (19:39). That is the last time he is mentioned in Scripture.

7:51 Nicodemus confronted the Pharisees with their failure to keep their own laws. The Pharisees were losing ground—the Temple guards came back impressed by Jesus (7:46), and one of the Pharisees' own, Nicodemus, was defending him. With their hypocritical motives being exposed and their prestige slowly eroding, they began to move to protect themselves. Pride would interfere with their ability to reason, and soon they would become obsessed with getting rid of Jesus just to save face. What was good and right no longer mattered.

7:52
Isa 9:1-2
Matt 4:14-16
John 1:46

⁵²They replied, "Are you from Galilee, too? Search the Scriptures and see for yourself—no prophet ever comes from Galilee!"

[The most ancient Greek manuscripts do not include John 7:53–8:11.]

Jesus Forgives an Adulterous Woman (**125**)
⁵³Then the meeting broke up and everybody went home.

8:2
Matt 26:55

8 Jesus returned to the Mount of Olives, ²but early the next morning he was back again at the Temple. A crowd soon gathered, and he sat down and taught them. ³As he was speaking, the teachers of religious law and Pharisees brought a woman they had caught in the act of adultery. They put her in front of the crowd.

⁴"Teacher," they said to Jesus, "this woman was caught in the very act of adultery. ⁵The law of Moses says to stone her. What do you say?"

8:5
Lev 20:10
Deut 22:22-24
Job 31:11
8:6
Matt 22:15
8:7
Deut 17:7

⁶They were trying to trap him into saying something they could use against him, but Jesus stooped down and wrote in the dust with his finger. ⁷They kept demanding an answer, so he stood up again and said, "All right, stone her. But let those who have never sinned throw the first stones!" ⁸Then he stooped down again and wrote in the dust.

⁹When the accusers heard this, they slipped away one by one, beginning with the oldest, until only Jesus was left in the middle of the crowd with the woman. ¹⁰Then Jesus stood up again and said to her, "Where are your accusers? Didn't even one of them condemn you?"

8:11
John 5:14

¹¹"No, Lord," she said.

And Jesus said, "Neither do I. Go and sin no more."

8:12
Isa 9:1-2
John 1:4-5, 9; 3:19;
9:5; 12:35-36, 46
2 Cor 4:6

Jesus Is the Light of the World (**126**)
¹²Jesus said to the people, "I am the light of the world. If you follow me, you won't be stumbling through the darkness, because you will have the light that leads to life."

¹³The Pharisees replied, "You are making false claims about yourself!"

8:3-6 The Jewish leaders had already disregarded the law by arresting the woman without the man. The law required that both parties to adultery be stoned (Leviticus 20:10; Deuteronomy 22:22). The leaders were using the woman as a trap so they could trick Jesus. If Jesus said the woman should not be stoned, they would accuse him of violating Moses' law. If he urged them to execute her, they would report him to the Romans, who did not permit the Jews to carry out their own executions (18:31).

8:7 This is a significant statement about judging others. Because Jesus upheld the legal penalty for adultery, stoning, he could not be accused of being against the law. But by saying that only a sinless person could throw the first stone, he highlighted the importance of compassion and forgiveness. When others are caught in sin, are you quick to pass judgment? To do so is to act as though you have never sinned. It is God's role to judge, not ours. Our role is to show forgiveness and compassion.

8:8 It is uncertain whether Jesus was merely ignoring the accusers by writing on the ground, listing their sins, or writing out the Ten Commandments.

8:9 When Jesus said that only someone who had not sinned should throw the first stone, the leaders slipped quietly away, from oldest to youngest. Evidently the older men were more aware of their sins than the younger. Age and experience often temper youthful self-righteousness. But whatever your age, take an honest look at your life. Recognize your sinful nature, and look for ways to help others rather than hurt them.

8:11 Jesus didn't condemn the woman accused of adultery, but neither did he ignore or condone her sin. He told her to leave her life of sin. Jesus stands ready to forgive any sin in your life, but confession and repentance mean a change of heart. With God's help we can accept Christ's forgiveness and stop our wrongdoing.

8:12 To understand what Jesus meant by "the light of the world," see the note on 1:4, 5.

8:12 Jesus was speaking in the part of the Temple where the offerings were put (8:20), where candles burned to symbolize the pillar of fire that led the people of Israel through the wilderness (Exodus 13:21, 22). In this context, Jesus called himself the light of the world. The pillar of fire represented God's presence, protection, and guidance. Jesus brings God's presence, protection, and guidance. Is he the light of *your* world?

8:12 What does it mean to follow Christ? As a soldier follows his captain, so we should follow Christ, our commander. As a slave follows his master, so we should follow Christ, our Lord. As we follow the advice of a trusted counselor, so we should follow Jesus' commands to us in Scripture. As we follow the laws of our nation, so we should follow the laws of the Kingdom of Heaven.

8:13, 14 The Pharisees thought Jesus was either a lunatic or a liar. Jesus provided them with a third alternative: He was telling the truth. Because most of the Pharisees refused to consider the third alternative, they never recognized him as Messiah and Lord. If you are seeking to know who Jesus is, do not close any door before looking through it honestly. Only with an open mind will you know the truth that he is Messiah and Lord.

8:13-18 The Pharisees argued that Jesus' claim was legally invalid because he had no other witnesses. Jesus responded that his confirming witness was God himself. Jesus and the Father made two witnesses, the number required by the law (Deuteronomy 19:15).

¹⁴Jesus told them, "These claims are valid even though I make them about myself. For I know where I came from and where I am going, but you don't know this about me. ¹⁵You judge me with all your human limitations,* but I am not judging anyone. ¹⁶And if I did, my judgment would be correct in every respect because I am not alone—I have with me the Father who sent me. ¹⁷Your own law says that if two people agree about something, their witness is accepted as fact.* ¹⁸I am one witness, and my Father who sent me is the other."

¹⁹"Where is your father?" they asked.

Jesus answered, "Since you don't know who I am, you don't know who my Father is. If you knew me, then you would know my Father, too." ²⁰Jesus made these statements while he was teaching in the section of the Temple known as the Treasury. But he was not arrested, because his time had not yet come.

Jesus Warns of Coming Judgment (127)

²¹Later Jesus said to them again, "I am going away. You will search for me and die in your sin. You cannot come where I am going."

²²The Jewish leaders asked, "Is he planning to commit suicide? What does he mean, 'You cannot come where I am going'?"

²³Then he said to them, "You are from below; I am from above. You are of this world; I am not. ²⁴That is why I said that you will die in your sins; for unless you believe that I am who I say I am, you will die in your sins."

²⁵"Tell us who you are," they demanded.

Jesus replied, "I am the one I have always claimed to be.* ²⁶I have much to say about you and much to condemn, but I won't. For I say only what I have heard from the one who sent me, and he is true." ²⁷But they still didn't understand that he was talking to them about his Father.

²⁸So Jesus said, "When you have lifted up the Son of Man on the cross, then you will realize that I am he and that I do nothing on my own, but I speak what the Father taught me. ²⁹And the one who sent me is with me—he has not deserted me. For I always do those things that are pleasing to him." ³⁰Then many who heard him say these things believed in him.

Jesus Speaks about God's True Children (128)

³¹Jesus said to the people* who believed in him, "You are truly my disciples if you keep obeying my teachings. ³²And you will know the truth, and the truth will set you free."

³³"But we are descendants of Abraham," they said. "We have never been slaves to anyone on earth. What do you mean, 'set free'?"

³⁴Jesus replied, "I assure you that everyone who sins is a slave of sin. ³⁵A slave is not a permanent member of the family, but a son is part of the family forever. ³⁶So if the Son sets you free, you will indeed be free. ³⁷Yes, I realize that you are descendants of Abraham. And yet some of you are trying to kill me because my message does not find a place in your hearts. ³⁸I am telling you what I saw when I was with my Father. But you are following the advice of your father."

³⁹"Our father is Abraham," they declared.

8:15 Or *judge me by human standards.* **8:17** See Deut 19:15. **8:25** Or *"Why do I speak to you at all?"* **8:31** Greek *Jewish people;* also in 8:48, 52, 57.

8:14
John 7:28; 9:29

8:16
John 5:30

8:17-18
Deut 17:6; 19:15
John 5:37
1 Jn 5:7-9

8:19
John 14:7, 9

8:20
Mark 12:41
John 7:30

8:21
John 7:34, 36;
13:33

8:22
John 7:35

8:23
John 3:31; 17:14

8:24
Exod 3:14-15
John 4:26; 8:28,
58; 13:19

8:26
John 3:32-34; 12:49

8:28
John 3:14; 5:19;
8:24; 12:32

8:29
John 4:34; 6:38;
8:16; 14:10; 16:32

8:30
John 7:31

8:31
John 15:7
2 Jn 1:9

8:32
Rom 8:2
2 Cor 3:17
Gal 5:1, 13

8:33
Matt 3:9
Luke 3:8

8:34
Rom 6:16, 20
2 Pet 2:19

8:35
Gen 21:10
Gal 4:30

8:20 The Temple Treasury was located in the Court of Women. In this area, 13 collection boxes were set up to receive money offerings. Seven of the boxes were for the Temple tax; the other 6 were for freewill offerings. On another occasion, a widow placed her money in one of these boxes, and Jesus taught a profound lesson from her action (Luke 21:1-4).

8:24 People will die in their sins if they reject Christ, because they are rejecting the only way to be rescued from sin. Sadly, many are so taken up with the values of this world that they are blind to the priceless gift Christ offers. Where are you looking? Don't focus on this world's values and miss what is most valuable—eternal life with God.

8:32 Jesus himself is the truth that sets us free (8:36). He is the source of truth, the perfect standard of what is right. He frees us from the consequences of sin, from self-deception, and from deception by Satan. He shows us clearly the way to eternal life with God. Thus, Jesus does not give us freedom to do what we want, but freedom to follow God. As we seek to serve God, Jesus' perfect truth frees us to be all that God meant us to be.

8:34, 35 Sin has a way of enslaving us, controlling us, dominating us, and dictating our actions. Jesus can free you from this slavery that keeps you from becoming the person God created you to be. If sin is restraining, mastering, or enslaving you, Jesus can break its power over your life.

8:39
Matt 3:9
John 8:33
Gal 3:7, 14, 29

8:41
Deut 32:6
Isa 63:16; 64:8
Mal 1:6

8:42
1 Jn 5:1

8:44
Gen 3:4; 4:9
1 Jn 3:8

8:45
John 18:37

8:47
1 Jn 4:6

"No," Jesus replied, "for if you were children of Abraham, you would follow his good example.* 40I told you the truth I heard from God, but you are trying to kill me. Abraham wouldn't do a thing like that. 41No, you are obeying your real father when you act that way."

They replied, "We were not born out of wedlock! Our true Father is God himself."

42Jesus told them, "If God were your Father, you would love me, because I have come to you from God. I am not here on my own, but he sent me. 43Why can't you understand what I am saying? It is because you are unable to do so! 44For you are the children of your father the Devil, and you love to do the evil things he does. He was a murderer from the beginning and has always hated the truth. There is no truth in him. When he lies, it is consistent with his character; for he is a liar and the father of lies. 45So when I tell the truth, you just naturally don't believe me! 46Which of you can truthfully accuse me of sin? And since I am telling you the truth, why don't you believe me? 47Anyone whose Father is God listens gladly to the words of God. Since you don't, it proves you aren't God's children."

Jesus States He Is Eternal (129)

48The people retorted, "You Samaritan devil! Didn't we say all along that you were possessed by a demon?"

8:50
John 5:41

8:51
John 5:24; 11:25,
26

8:53
John 4:12

8:54
John 16:14; 17:5

8:55
John 7:28-29; 15:10

8:56
Gen 18:18;
22:17-18
Matt 13:17
Heb 11:13

8:58
Exod 3:14
Isa 43:10, 13
John 1:1; 8:24, 28

49"No," Jesus said, "I have no demon in me. For I honor my Father—and you dishonor me. 50And though I have no wish to glorify myself, God wants to glorify me. Let him be the judge. 51I assure you, anyone who obeys my teaching will never die!"

52The people said, "Now we know you are possessed by a demon. Even Abraham and the prophets died, but you say that those who obey your teaching will never die! 53Are you greater than our father Abraham, who died? Are you greater than the prophets, who died? Who do you think you are?"

54Jesus answered, "If I am merely boasting about myself, it doesn't count. But it is my Father who says these glorious things about me. You say, 'He is our God,' 55but you do not even know him. I know him. If I said otherwise, I would be as great a liar as you! But it is true—I know him and obey him. 56Your ancestor Abraham rejoiced as he looked forward to my coming. He saw it and was glad."

57The people said, "You aren't even fifty years old. How can you say you have seen Abraham?*"

58Jesus answered, "The truth is, I existed before Abraham was even born!"*

8:39 Some manuscripts read *if you are children of Abraham, follow his example.*   **8:57** Some manuscripts read *How can you say Abraham has seen you?*   **8:58** Or *"Truly, truly, before Abraham was, I am."*

8:41 Jesus made a distinction between hereditary children and *true* children. The religious leaders were hereditary children of Abraham (founder of the Jewish nation) and therefore claimed to be children of God. But their actions showed them to be true children of Satan, for they lived under Satan's guidance. True children of Abraham (faithful followers of God) would not act as they did. Your church membership and family connections will not make you a true child of God. Your true father is the one you imitate and obey.

8:43 The religious leaders were unable to understand because they refused to listen. Satan used their stubbornness, pride, and prejudices to keep them from believing in Jesus.

8:44, 45 The attitudes and actions of these leaders clearly identified them as followers of Satan. They may not have been conscious of this, but their hatred of truth, their lies, and their murderous intentions indicated how much control the Devil had over them. They were his tools in carrying out his plans; they spoke the very same language of lies. Satan still uses people to obstruct God's work (Genesis 4:8; Romans 5:12; 1 John 3:12).

8:46 No one could accuse Jesus of a single sin. People who hated him and wanted him dead scrutinized his behavior but could find nothing wrong. Jesus proved he was God in the flesh by his sinless life. He is the only perfect example for us to follow.

8:46, 47 In a number of places Jesus intentionally challenged his listeners to test him. He welcomed those who wanted to

question his claims and character as long as they were willing to follow through on what they discovered. Jesus' challenge clarifies the two most frequent reasons that people miss when encountering him: (1) They never accept his challenge to test him, or (2) they test him but are not willing to believe what they discover. Have you made either of those mistakes?

8:51 When Jesus says those who obey won't die, he is talking about spiritual death, not physical death. Even physical death, however, will eventually be overcome. Those who follow Christ will be raised to live eternally with him.

8:56 God told Abraham, the father of the Jewish nation, that through him all nations would be blessed (Genesis 12:1-7; 15:1-21). Abraham had been able to see this through the eyes of faith. Jesus, a descendant of Abraham, blessed all people through his death, resurrection, and offer of salvation.

8:58 This is one of the most powerful statements uttered by Jesus. When he said that he existed before Abraham was born, he undeniably proclaimed his divinity. Not only did Jesus say that he existed before Abraham; he also applied God's holy name (*I AM*—Exodus 3:14) to himself (see NLT text note). This claim demands a response. It cannot be ignored. The Jewish leaders tried to stone Jesus for blasphemy because he claimed equality with God. But Jesus *is* God. How have you responded to Jesus, the Son of God?

[59]At that point they picked up stones to kill him. But Jesus hid himself from them and left the Temple.

Jesus Heals the Man Who Was Born Blind (**148**)

9 As Jesus was walking along, he saw a man who had been blind from birth. [2]"Teacher," his disciples asked him, "why was this man born blind? Was it a result of his own sins or those of his parents?"

[3]"It was not because of his sins or his parents' sins," Jesus answered. "He was born blind so the power of God could be seen in him. [4]All of us must quickly carry out the tasks assigned us by the one who sent me, because there is little time left before the night falls and all work comes to an end. [5]But while I am still here in the world, I am the light of the world."

[6]Then he spit on the ground, made mud with the saliva, and smoothed the mud over the blind man's eyes. [7]He told him, "Go and wash in the pool of Siloam" (Siloam means Sent). So the man went and washed, and came back seeing!

[8]His neighbors and others who knew him as a blind beggar asked each other, "Is this the same man—that beggar?" [9]Some said he was, and others said, "No, but he surely looks like him!"

And the beggar kept saying, "I am the same man!"

[10]They asked, "Who healed you? What happened?"

[11]He told them, "The man they call Jesus made mud and smoothed it over my eyes and told me, 'Go to the pool of Siloam and wash off the mud.' I went and washed, and now I can see!"

[12]"Where is he now?" they asked.

"I don't know," he replied.

Religious Leaders Question the Blind Man (**149**)

[13]Then they took the man to the Pharisees. [14]Now as it happened, Jesus had healed the man on a Sabbath. [15]The Pharisees asked the man all about it. So he told them, "He smoothed the mud over my eyes, and when it was washed away, I could see!"

[16]Some of the Pharisees said, "This man Jesus is not from God, for he is working on the Sabbath." Others said, "But how could an ordinary sinner do such miraculous signs?" So there was a deep division of opinion among them.

[17]Then the Pharisees once again questioned the man who had been blind and demanded, "This man who opened your eyes—who do you say he is?"

The man replied, "I think he must be a prophet."

[18]The Jewish leaders wouldn't believe he had been blind, so they called in his parents. [19]They asked them, "Is this your son? Was he born blind? If so, how can he see?"

9:2
Exod 20:5
Ezek 18:20
Luke 13:2
John 9:34

9:3
John 11:4

9:4
John 5:17; 11:9;
12:35

9:5
Isa 49:6
John 1:4-5, 9; 8:12;
12:46

9:6
Mark 8:23

9:7
2 Kgs 5:10
Isa 35:5

9::8
Acts 3:10

9:14
Luke 13:14
John 5:9

9:16
John 3:2; 7:43

9:17
Matt 21:11

8:59 In accordance with the law given in Leviticus 24:16, the religious leaders were ready to stone Jesus for claiming to be God. They well understood what Jesus was claiming, and because they didn't believe he was God, they charged him with blasphemy. It is ironic that *they* were really the blasphemers, cursing and attacking the very God they claimed to serve!

9:1ff In chapter 9, we see four different reactions to Jesus. The neighbors revealed surprise and skepticism; the Pharisees showed disbelief and prejudice; the parents believed but kept quiet for fear of excommunication; and the healed man showed consistent, growing faith.

9:2, 3 A common belief in Jewish culture was that calamity or suffering was the result of some great sin. But Christ used this man's suffering to teach about faith and to glorify God. We live in a fallen world where good behavior is not always rewarded and bad behavior not always punished. Therefore, innocent people sometimes suffer. If God took suffering away whenever we asked, we would follow him for comfort and convenience, not out of love and devotion. Regardless of the reasons for our suffering, Jesus has the power to help us deal with it. When you suffer from a disease, tragedy, or disability, try not to ask, Why

did this happen to me? or What did I do wrong? Instead, ask God to give you strength for the trial and a clearer perspective on what is happening.

9:7 The pool of Siloam was built by Hezekiah. His workers constructed an underground tunnel from a spring outside the city walls to carry water into the city. Thus, the people could always get water without fear of being attacked. This was especially important during times of siege (see 2 Kings 20:20; 2 Chronicles 32:30).

9:13-17 While the Pharisees conducted investigations and debated about Jesus, people were being healed and lives were being changed. The Pharisees' skepticism was based not on insufficient evidence, but on jealousy of Jesus' popularity and his influence on the people.

9:14-16 The Jewish Sabbath, Saturday, was the weekly holy day of rest. The Pharisees had made a long list of specific dos and don'ts regarding the Sabbath. Kneading the clay and healing the man were considered work and therefore were forbidden. Jesus may have purposely made the clay in order to emphasize his teaching about the Sabbath—that it is right to care for others' needs even if it involves working on a day of rest.

9:22
Luke 6:22
John 7:13; 12:42;
16:2; 19:38
Acts 5:13

9:24
Josh 7:19

9:28
John 5:45

9:29
John 8:14

9:31
Job 27:8-9
Pss 34:15; 66:18;
145:19
Prov 15:29
Isa 1:15
Jer 11:11; 14:12
Mic 3:4
Zech 7:13

9:33
John 3:2

9:34
John 9:2

9:37
John 4:26

9:39
Luke 4:18

9:40
Rom 2:19

9:41
John 15:22

²⁰His parents replied, "We know this is our son and that he was born blind, ²¹but we don't know how he can see or who healed him. He is old enough to speak for himself. Ask him." ²²They said this because they were afraid of the Jewish leaders, who had announced that anyone saying Jesus was the Messiah would be expelled from the synagogue. ²³That's why they said, "He is old enough to speak for himself. Ask him."

²⁴So for the second time they called in the man who had been blind and told him, "Give glory to God by telling the truth,* because we know Jesus is a sinner."

²⁵"I don't know whether he is a sinner," the man replied. "But I know this: I was blind, and now I can see!"

²⁶"But what did he do?" they asked. "How did he heal you?"

²⁷"Look!" the man exclaimed. "I told you once. Didn't you listen? Why do you want to hear it again? Do you want to become his disciples, too?"

²⁸Then they cursed him and said, "You are his disciple, but we are disciples of Moses. ²⁹We know God spoke to Moses, but as for this man, we don't know anything about him."

³⁰"Why, that's very strange!" the man replied. "He healed my eyes, and yet you don't know anything about him! ³¹Well, God doesn't listen to sinners, but he is ready to hear those who worship him and do his will. ³²Never since the world began has anyone been able to open the eyes of someone born blind. ³³If this man were not from God, he couldn't do it."

³⁴"You were born in sin!" they answered. "Are you trying to teach us?" And they threw him out of the synagogue.

Jesus Teaches about Spiritual Blindness (**150**)

³⁵When Jesus heard what had happened, he found the man and said, "Do you believe in the Son of Man*?"

³⁶The man answered, "Who is he, sir, because I would like to."

³⁷"You have seen him," Jesus said, "and he is speaking to you!"

³⁸"Yes, Lord," the man said, "I believe!" And he worshiped Jesus.

³⁹Then Jesus told him, "I have come to judge the world. I have come to give sight to the blind and to show those who think they see that they are blind."

⁴⁰The Pharisees who were standing there heard him and asked, "Are you saying we are blind?"

⁴¹"If you were blind, you wouldn't be guilty," Jesus replied. "But you remain guilty because you claim you can see."

9:24 Or *Give glory to God, not to Jesus;* Greek reads *Give glory to God.*   **9:35** Some manuscripts read *the Son of God.*

9:25 By now the man who had been blind had heard the same questions over and over. He did not know how or why he was healed, but he knew that his life had been miraculously changed, and he was not afraid to tell the truth. You don't need to know all the answers in order to share Christ with others. It is important to tell them how he has changed your life. Then trust that God will use your words to help others believe in him, too.

9:28, 34 The man's new faith was severely tested by some of the authorities. He was cursed and evicted from the synagogue. Persecution may come when you follow Jesus. You may lose friends; you may even lose your life. But no one can ever take away the eternal life that Jesus gives you.

9:38 The longer this man experienced his new life through Christ, the more confident he became in the one who had healed him. He gained not only physical sight but also spiritual sight as he recognized Jesus first as a prophet (9:17), then as his Lord. When you turn to Christ, you begin to see him differently. The longer you walk with him, the better you will understand who he is. Peter tells us to "grow in the special favor and knowledge of our Lord and Savior Jesus Christ" (2 Peter 3:18). If you want to know more about Jesus, keep walking with him.

9:40, 41 The Pharisees were shocked that Jesus thought they were spiritually blind. Jesus countered by saying that it was only blindness (stubbornness and stupidity) that could excuse their behavior. To those who remained open and recognized how sin had truly blinded them from knowing the truth, he gave spiritual understanding and insight. But he rejected those who had become complacent, self-satisfied, and blind.

Jesus Is the Good Shepherd (**151**)

10 "I assure you, anyone who sneaks over the wall of a sheepfold, rather than going through the gate, must surely be a thief and a robber! ²For a shepherd enters through the gate. ³The gatekeeper opens the gate for him, and the sheep hear his voice and come to him. He calls his own sheep by name and leads them out. ⁴After he has gathered his own flock, he walks ahead of them, and they follow him because they recognize his voice. ⁵They won't follow a stranger; they will run from him because they don't recognize his voice."

⁶Those who heard Jesus use this illustration didn't understand what he meant, ⁷so he explained it to them. "I assure you, I am the gate for the sheep," he said. ⁸"All others who came before me were thieves and robbers. But the true sheep did not listen to them. ⁹Yes, I am the gate. Those who come in through me will be saved. Wherever they go, they will find green pastures. ¹⁰The thief's purpose is to steal and kill and destroy. My purpose is to give life in all its fullness.

¹¹"I am the good shepherd. The good shepherd lays down his life for the sheep. ¹²A hired hand will run when he sees a wolf coming. He will leave the sheep because they aren't his and he isn't their shepherd. And so the wolf attacks them and scatters the flock. ¹³The hired hand runs away because he is merely hired and has no real concern for the sheep.

¹⁴"I am the good shepherd; I know my own sheep, and they know me, ¹⁵just as my Father knows me and I know the Father. And I lay down my life for the sheep. ¹⁶I have other sheep, too, that are not in this sheepfold. I must bring them also, and they will listen to my voice; and there will be one flock with one shepherd.

¹⁷"The Father loves me because I lay down my life that I may have it back again. ¹⁸No one can take my life from me. I lay down my life voluntarily. For I have the right to lay it down when I want to and also the power to take it again. For my Father has given me this command."

¹⁹When he said these things, the people* were again divided in their opinions about him. ²⁰Some of them said, "He has a demon, or he's crazy. Why listen to a man like that?"

10:19 Greek *Jewish people.*

10:2
Acts 20:28

10:4
Ps 80:2
John 10:27

10:6
John 16:25

10:7
John 14:6

10:8
Jer 23:1-2
Ezek 34:2-3

10:9
Ps 118:20
John 14:6

10:10
John 5:40
Acts 20:29
2 Pet 2:1

10:11
Isa 40:11
Ezek 34:11-16, 23
Heb 13:20
1 Pet 2:25
1 Jn 3:16
Rev 7:17

10:14
2 Tim 2:19

10:15
Matt 11:27

10:16
Isa 56:8
Ezek 37:24
John 11:52
Eph 2:14-18

10:17-18
Phil 2:8-9
Heb 5:8; 7:16

10:1 At night, sheep were often gathered into a sheepfold to protect them from thieves, weather, or wild animals. The sheepfolds were caves, sheds, or open areas surrounded by walls made of stones or branches. The shepherd often slept in the fold to protect the sheep. Just as a shepherd cares for his sheep, Jesus, the good shepherd, cares for his flock (those who follow him). The prophet Ezekiel, in predicting the coming of the Messiah, called him a shepherd (Ezekiel 34:23).

MINISTRY EAST OF THE JORDAN Jesus had been in Jerusalem for the Festival of Shelters (7:2); then he preached in various towns, probably in Judea, before returning to Jerusalem for Hanukkah. He again angered the religious leaders, who tried to arrest him, but he left the city and went to the region east of the Jordan to preach.

10:7 In the sheepfold, the shepherd functioned as a gate, letting the sheep in and protecting them. Jesus is the gate to God's salvation for us. He offers access to safety and security. Christ is our protector. Some people resent that Jesus is the gate, the only way of access to God. But Jesus is God's Son—why should we seek any other way or want to customize a different approach to God? (See also the notes on 14:6.)

10:10 In contrast to the thief who takes life, Jesus gives life. The life he gives right now is abundantly rich and full. It is eternal, yet it begins immediately. Life in Christ is lived on a higher plane because of his overflowing forgiveness, love, and guidance. Have you taken Christ's offer of life?

10:11, 12 A hired hand tends the sheep for money, while the shepherd does it out of love. The shepherd owns the sheep and is committed to them. Jesus is not merely doing a job; he is committed to love us and even lay down his life for us. False teachers and false prophets do not have this commitment.

10:16 The "other sheep" were non-Jews. Jesus came to save Gentiles as well as Jews. This is an insight into his worldwide mission—to die for the sins of the world. People tend to want to restrict God's blessings to their own group, but Jesus refuses to be limited by the fences we build.

10:17, 18 Jesus' death and resurrection, as part of God's plan for the salvation of the world, were under God's full control. No one could kill Jesus without his consent.

10:19, 20 If Jesus had been merely a man, his claims to be God would have proven him insane. But his miracles proved his words true—he really was God. The Jewish leaders could not see beyond their own prejudices, and they looked at Jesus only from a human perspective—Jesus confined in a human box. But Jesus was not limited by their restricted vision.

²¹ Others said, "This doesn't sound like a man possessed by a demon! Can a demon open the eyes of the blind?"

Religious Leaders Surround Jesus at the Temple (**152**)

²² It was now winter, and Jesus was in Jerusalem at the time of Hanukkah.* ²³ He was at the Temple, walking through the section known as Solomon's Colonnade. ²⁴ The Jewish leaders surrounded him and asked, "How long are you going to keep us in suspense? If you are the Messiah, tell us plainly."

²⁵ Jesus replied, "I have already told you, and you don't believe me. The proof is what I do in the name of my Father. ²⁶ But you don't believe me because you are not part of my flock. ²⁷ My sheep recognize my voice; I know them, and they follow me. ²⁸ I give them eternal life, and they will never perish. No one will snatch them away from me, ²⁹ for my Father has given them to me, and he is more powerful than anyone else. So no one can take them from me. ³⁰ The Father and I are one."

³¹ Once again the Jewish leaders picked up stones to kill him. ³² Jesus said, "At my Father's direction I have done many things to help the people. For which one of these good deeds are you killing me?"

10:22 Or *the Festival of Dedication.*

10:23 Acts 3:11; 5:12
10:24 Luke 22:67
10:25 John 5:36; 10:38; 14:11
10:26 John 8:47
10:28 John 6:37, 39; 17:12
10:29 John 14:28 17:2, 6, 24
10:30 John 1:1; 10:38; 14:8-11; 17:21-24

THE NAMES OF JESUS
In different settings, Jesus gave himself names that pointed to special roles he was ready to fulfill for people. Some of these refer back to the Old Testament promises of the Messiah. Others were ways to help people understand him.

Reference	Name	Significance
6:27	Son of Man	Jesus' favorite reference to himself. It emphasized his humanity—but the way he used it, it was a claim to divinity.
6:35	Bread of life	Refers to his life-giving role—that he is the only source of eternal life.
8:12	Light of the world	Light is a symbol of spiritual truth. Jesus is the universal answer for people's need of spiritual truth.
10:7	Gate for the sheep	Jesus is the only way into God's Kingdom.
10:11	Good shepherd	Jesus appropriated the prophetic images of the Messiah pictured in the Old Testament. This is a claim to divinity, focusing on Jesus' love and guidance.
11:25	The resurrection and the life	Not only is Jesus the source of life; he is the power over death.
14:6	The way, the truth, and the life	Jesus is the method, the message, and the meaning for all people. With this title, he summarized his purpose in coming to earth.
15:1	The true vine	This title has an important second part, "you are the branches." As in so many of his other names, Jesus reminds us that just as branches gain life from the vine and cannot live apart from it, so we are completely dependent on Christ for spiritual life.

10:22, 23 Hanukkah commemorated the cleansing of the Temple under Judas Maccabeus in 164 B.C. after Antiochus Epiphanes had defiled it by sacrificing a pig on the altar of burnt offering. The festival was celebrated toward the end of December.

10:23 Solomon's Colonnade was a roofed walkway supported by large stone columns, just inside the walls of the Temple courtyard.

10:24 Many people asking for proof do so for the wrong reasons. Most of these questioners didn't want to follow Jesus in the way that he wanted to lead them. They hoped that Jesus would declare himself Messiah for perverted reasons. They, along with the disciples and everyone else in the Jewish nation, would have been delighted to have him drive out the Romans. Many of them didn't think he was going to do that, however. These doubters hoped he would identify himself so they could accuse him of telling lies (as the Pharisees did in 8:13).

10:28, 29 Just as a shepherd protects his sheep, Jesus protects his people from eternal harm. While believers can expect to suffer on earth, Satan cannot harm their souls or take away their eternal life with God. There are many reasons to be afraid here on earth because this is the Devil's domain (1 Peter 5:8). But if you choose to follow Jesus, he will give you everlasting safety.

10:30 This is the clearest statement of Jesus' divinity he ever made. Jesus and his Father are not the same person, but they are one in essence and nature. Thus, Jesus is not merely a good teacher—he is God. His claim to be God was unmistakable. The religious leaders wanted to kill him because their laws said that anyone claiming to be God should die. Nothing could persuade them that Jesus' claim was true.

10:31 The Jewish leaders attempted to carry out the directive found in Leviticus 24:16 regarding those who blaspheme (claim to be God). They intended to stone Jesus.

33 They replied, "Not for any good work, but for blasphemy, because you, a mere man, have made yourself God."

34 Jesus replied, "It is written in your own law that God said to certain leaders of the people, 'I say, you are gods!' * 35 And you know that the Scriptures cannot be altered. So if those people, who received God's message, were called 'gods,' 36 why do you call it blasphemy when the Holy One who was sent into the world by the Father says, 'I am the Son of God'? 37 Don't believe me unless I carry out my Father's work. 38 But if I do his work, believe in what I have done, even if you don't believe me. Then you will realize that the Father is in me, and I am in the Father."

39 Once again they tried to arrest him, but he got away and left them. 40 He went beyond the Jordan River to stay near the place where John was first baptizing. 41 And many followed him. "John didn't do miracles," they remarked to one another, "but all his predictions about this man have come true." 42 And many believed in him there.

3. Jesus encounters crucial events in Jerusalem

Lazarus Becomes Ill and Dies (165)

11 A man named Lazarus was sick. He lived in Bethany with his sisters, Mary and Martha. 2 This is the Mary who poured the expensive perfume on the Lord's feet and wiped them with her hair.* Her brother, Lazarus, was sick. 3 So the two sisters sent a message to Jesus telling him, "Lord, the one you love is very sick."

4 But when Jesus heard about it he said, "Lazarus's sickness will not end in death. No, it is for the glory of God. I, the Son of God, will receive glory from this." 5 Although Jesus loved Martha, Mary, and Lazarus, 6 he stayed where he was for the next two days and did not go to them. 7 Finally after two days, he said to his disciples, "Let's go to Judea again."

8 But his disciples objected. "Teacher," they said, "only a few days ago the Jewish leaders in Judea were trying to kill you. Are you going there again?"

9 Jesus replied, "There are twelve hours of daylight every day. As long as it is light, people can walk safely. They can see because they have the light of this world. 10 Only at night is there danger of stumbling because there is no light." 11 Then he said, "Our friend Lazarus has fallen asleep, but now I will go and wake him up."

10:34 Ps 82:6.   11:2 This incident is recorded in chapter 12.

10:33
Lev 24:16
Matt 26:63-66
John 1:1, 18; 5:18;
20:28
Rom 9:5
Phil 2:6
Titus 2:13
2 Pet 1:1
1 Jn 5:20

10:34
†Ps 82:6

10:36
John 5:17-20

10:42
John 2:23; 7:31;
8:30; 11:45; 12:11,
42

11:1
Matt 21:17
Luke 10:38

11:2
John 12:3

11:4
John 9:3

11:8
John 8:59; 10:31

11:9
John 9:4

11:10
John 12:35

11:11
Dan 12:2
Matt 9:24; 27:52
Mark 5:39
Luke 8:52
Acts 7:60
1 Cor 11:30

10:34-36 Jesus referred to Psalm 82:6, where the Israelite rulers and judges are called "gods" (see also Exodus 4:16; 7:1). If God called the Israelite leaders gods because they were agents of God's revelation and will, how could it be blasphemy for Jesus to call himself the Son of God? Jesus was rebuking the religious leaders, because he is the Son of God in a unique, unparalleled relationship of oneness with the Father.

10:35 "The Scriptures cannot be altered" is a clear statement of the truth of the Bible. If we accept Christ as Lord, we also must accept his testimony to the Bible as God's Word.

11:1 The village of Bethany was located about two miles east of Jerusalem on the road to Jericho. It was near enough to Jerusalem for Jesus and the disciples to be in danger, but far enough away so as not to attract attention prematurely.

11:3 As their brother grew very sick, Mary and Martha turned to Jesus for help. They believed in his ability to help because they had seen his miracles. We, too, know of Jesus' miracles, both from Scripture and through changed lives we have seen. When we need extraordinary help, Jesus offers extraordinary resources. We should not hesitate to ask him for assistance.

11:4 Any trial a believer faces can ultimately bring glory to God because God can bring good out of any bad situation (Genesis 50:20; Romans 8:28). When trouble comes, do you grumble, complain, and blame God, or do you see your problems as opportunities to honor him?

11:5-7 Jesus loved this family and often stayed with them. He knew their pain but did not respond immediately. His delay had a specific purpose. God's timing, especially his delays, may make

us think he is not answering or is not answering the way we want. But he will meet all our needs according to his perfect schedule and purpose (Philippians 4:19). Patiently await his timing.

11:9, 10 "Daylight" symbolizes the knowledge of God's will, and "night," the absence of this knowledge. When we move ahead in darkness, we will be likely to stumble.

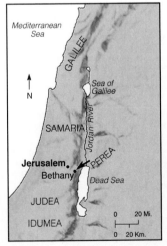

JESUS RAISES LAZARUS
Jesus had been preaching in the villages beyond the Jordan, probably in Perea, when he received the news of Lazarus's sickness. Jesus did not leave immediately, but waited two days before returning to Judea. He knew Lazarus would be dead when he arrived in Bethany, but he was going to do a great miracle.

¹² The disciples said, "Lord, if he is sleeping, that means he is getting better!" ¹³ They thought Jesus meant Lazarus was having a good night's rest, but Jesus meant Lazarus had died.

¹⁴ Then he told them plainly, "Lazarus is dead. ¹⁵ And for your sake, I am glad I wasn't there, because this will give you another opportunity to believe in me. Come, let's go see him."

¹⁶ Thomas, nicknamed the Twin,* said to his fellow disciples, "Let's go, too—and die with Jesus."

Jesus Comforts Mary and Martha (**166**)

¹⁷ When Jesus arrived at Bethany, he was told that Lazarus had already been in his grave for four days. ¹⁸ Bethany was only a few miles* down the road from Jerusalem, ¹⁹ and many of the people* had come to pay their respects and console Martha and Mary on their loss. ²⁰ When Martha got word that Jesus was coming, she went to meet him. But Mary stayed at home. ²¹ Martha said to Jesus, "Lord, if you had been here, my brother would not have died. ²² But even now I know that God will give you whatever you ask."

²³ Jesus told her, "Your brother will rise again."

²⁴ "Yes," Martha said, "when everyone else rises, on resurrection day."

²⁵ Jesus told her, "I am the resurrection and the life.* Those who believe in me, even though they die like everyone else, will live again. ²⁶ They are given eternal life for believing in me and will never perish. Do you believe this, Martha?"

11:16 Greek *the one who was called Didymus.*   **11:18** Greek *was about 15 stadia* [about 2.8 kilometers].
11:19 Greek *Jewish people;* also 11:31, 33, 36, 45, 54.   **11:25** Some manuscripts do not include *and the life.*

11:16
Matt 10:3
John 14:5;
20:24-28; 21:2
Acts 1:3

11:20
Luke 10:38-42

11:22
John 16:30

11:23-24
Dan 12:2
John 5:28-29
Acts 24:15
Phil 3:21
1 Thes 4:14

11:25
John 1:4; 3:36;
5:21; 6:39-40; 14:6
Col 1:18; 3:4
1 Jn 1:1-2; 5:10-11
Rev 1:17-18

11:26
John 8:51

GREAT EXPECTATIONS
Wherever he went, Jesus exceeded people's expectations.

What was expected	What Jesus did	Reference
A man looked for healing.	Jesus also forgave his sins.	Mark 2:1–12
The disciples were expecting an ordinary day of fishing.	They found the Savior.	Luke 5:1–11
A widow was resigned to bury her dead son.	Jesus restored her son to life.	Luke 7:11–17
The religious leaders wanted a miracle.	Jesus offered them the Creator of miracles.	Matthew 12:38–45
A woman who wanted to be healed touched Jesus.	Jesus helped her see it was her faith that had healed her.	Mark 5:25–34
The disciples thought the crowd should be sent home because there was no food.	Jesus used a small meal to feed thousands, and there were leftovers!	John 6:1–15
The crowds looked for a political leader to set up a new kingdom to overthrow Rome's control.	Jesus offered them an eternal, spiritual kingdom to overthrow sin's control.	A theme throughout the Gospels
The disciples wanted to eat the Passover meal with Jesus, their Master.	Jesus washed their feet, showing that he was also their servant.	John 13:1–20
The religious leaders wanted Jesus killed and got their wish.	But Jesus rose from the dead!	John 11:53; 19:30; 20:1–29

11:14, 15 If Jesus had been with Lazarus during the final moments of Lazarus's sickness, he might have healed him rather than let him die. But Lazarus died so that Jesus' power over death could be shown to his disciples and others. The raising of Lazarus was an essential display of his power, and the resurrection from the dead is a crucial belief of the Christian faith. Jesus not only raised himself from the dead (10:18), but he has the power to raise others.

11:16 We often remember Thomas as "the doubter," because he doubted Jesus' resurrection. But here he demonstrated love and courage. The disciples knew the dangers of going with Jesus to Jerusalem, and they tried to talk him out of it. Thomas merely expressed what all of them felt. When their objections failed, they were willing to go and even die with Jesus. They may not have understood why Jesus would be killed, but they were loyal. There are unknown dangers in doing God's work. It is wise to consider the high cost of being Jesus' disciple.

11:25, 26 Jesus has power over life and death as well as power to forgive sins. This is because he is the Creator of life (see 14:6). He who *is* life can surely restore life. Whoever believes in Christ has a spiritual life that death cannot conquer or diminish in any way. When we realize his power and how wonderful his offer to us really is, how can we not commit our lives to him? To those of us who believe, what wonderful assurance and certainty we have: "I will live again, and you will, too" (14:19).

²⁷"Yes, Lord," she told him. "I have always believed you are the Messiah, the Son of God, the one who has come into the world from God." ²⁸Then she left him and returned to Mary. She called Mary aside from the mourners and told her, "The Teacher is here and wants to see you." ²⁹So Mary immediately went to him.

11:27
Matt 16:16
John 6:14

³⁰Now Jesus had stayed outside the village, at the place where Martha met him. ³¹When the people who were at the house trying to console Mary saw her leave so hastily, they assumed she was going to Lazarus's grave to weep. So they followed her there. ³²When Mary arrived and saw Jesus, she fell down at his feet and said, "Lord, if you had been here, my brother would not have died."

³³When Jesus saw her weeping and saw the other people wailing with her, he was moved with indignation and was deeply troubled. ³⁴"Where have you put him?" he asked them.

They told him, "Lord, come and see." ³⁵Then Jesus wept. ³⁶The people who were standing nearby said, "See how much he loved him." ³⁷But some said, "This man healed a blind man. Why couldn't he keep Lazarus from dying?"

11:35
Luke 19:41

11:37
John 9:6-7

Jesus Raises Lazarus from the Dead (**167**)

³⁸And again Jesus was deeply troubled. Then they came to the grave. It was a cave with a stone rolled across its entrance. ³⁹"Roll the stone aside," Jesus told them.

11:39
John 11:17

But Martha, the dead man's sister, said, "Lord, by now the smell will be terrible because he has been dead for four days."

⁴⁰Jesus responded, "Didn't I tell you that you will see God's glory if you believe?" ⁴¹So they rolled the stone aside. Then Jesus looked up to heaven and said, "Father, thank you for hearing me. ⁴²You always hear me, but I said it out loud for the sake of all these people standing here, so they will believe you sent me." ⁴³Then Jesus shouted, "Lazarus, come out!" ⁴⁴And Lazarus came out, bound in graveclothes, his face wrapped in a headcloth. Jesus told them, "Unwrap him and let him go!"

11:41
Matt 11:25

11:42
John 12:30

11:43
Luke 7:14

Religious Leaders Plot to Kill Jesus (**168**)

⁴⁵Many of the people who were with Mary believed in Jesus when they saw this happen. ⁴⁶But some went to the Pharisees and told them what Jesus had done. ⁴⁷Then the leading priests and Pharisees called the high council* together to discuss the situation. "What are we going to do?" they asked each other. "This man certainly performs many

11:47
Matt 26:3-5

11:47 Greek *the Sanhedrin.*

11:27 Martha is best known for being too busy to sit down and talk with Jesus (Luke 10:38-42). But here we see her as a woman of deep faith. Her statement of faith is exactly the response that Jesus wants from us.

TIME WITH THE DISCIPLES
Lazarus's return to life became the last straw for the religious leaders, who were bent on killing Jesus. So Jesus stopped his public ministry and took his disciples away from Jerusalem to Ephraim. From there they returned to Galilee for a while (see the map in Luke 17).

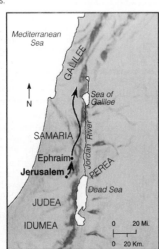

11:33-38 John stresses that we have a God who cares. This portrait contrasts with the Greek concept of God that was popular in that day—a God with no emotions and no messy involvement with humans. Here we see many of Jesus' emotions—compassion, indignation, sorrow, even frustration. He often expressed deep emotion, and we must never be afraid to reveal our true feelings to him. He understands them, for he experienced them. Be honest, and don't try to hide anything from your Savior. He cares.

11:35 When Jesus saw the weeping and wailing, he too wept openly. Perhaps he empathized with their grief, or perhaps he was troubled at their unbelief. In either case, Jesus showed that he cares enough for us to weep with us in our sorrow.

11:38 Tombs at this time were usually caves carved in the limestone rock of a hillside. A tomb was often large enough for people to walk inside. Several bodies would be placed in one tomb. After burial, a large stone was rolled across the entrance to the tomb.

11:44 Jesus raised others from the dead, including Jairus's daughter (Matthew 9:18-26; Mark 5:42, 43; Luke 8:40-56) and a widow's son (Luke 7:11-15).

11:45-53 Even when confronted point-blank with the power of Jesus' deity, some refused to believe. These eyewitnesses not only rejected Jesus; they plotted his murder. They were so hardened that they preferred to reject God's Son rather than admit that they were wrong. Beware of pride. If we allow it to grow, it can lead us into enormous sin.

miraculous signs. ⁴⁸If we leave him alone, the whole nation will follow him, and then the Roman army will come and destroy both our Temple and our nation."

⁴⁹And one of them, Caiaphas, who was high priest that year, said, "How can you be so stupid? ⁵⁰Why should the whole nation be destroyed? Let this one man die for the people."

⁵¹This prophecy that Jesus should die for the entire nation came from Caiaphas in his position as high priest. He didn't think of it himself; he was inspired to say it. ⁵²It was a prediction that Jesus' death would be not for Israel only, but for the gathering together of all the children of God scattered around the world.

⁵³So from that time on the Jewish leaders began to plot Jesus' death. ⁵⁴As a result, Jesus stopped his public ministry among the people and left Jerusalem. He went to a place near the wilderness, to the village of Ephraim, and stayed there with his disciples.

⁵⁵It was now almost time for the celebration of Passover, and many people from the country arrived in Jerusalem several days early so they could go through the cleansing ceremony before the Passover began. ⁵⁶They wanted to see Jesus, and as they talked in the Temple, they asked each other, "What do you think? Will he come for the Passover?" ⁵⁷Meanwhile, the leading priests and Pharisees had publicly announced that anyone seeing Jesus must report him immediately so they could arrest him.

A Woman Anoints Jesus with Perfume (**182**/Matthew 26:6-13; Mark 14:3-9)

12 Six days before the Passover ceremonies began, Jesus arrived in Bethany, the home of Lazarus—the man he had raised from the dead. ²A dinner was prepared in Jesus' honor. Martha served, and Lazarus sat at the table with him. ³Then Mary took a twelve-ounce jar* of expensive perfume made from essence of nard, and she anointed Jesus' feet with it and wiped his feet with her hair. And the house was filled with fragrance.

⁴But Judas Iscariot, one of his disciples—the one who would betray him—said, ⁵"That perfume was worth a small fortune.* It should have been sold and the money given to the poor." ⁶Not that he cared for the poor—he was a thief who was in charge of the disciples' funds, and he often took some for his own use.

⁷Jesus replied, "Leave her alone. She did it in preparation for my burial. ⁸You will always have the poor among you, but I will not be here with you much longer."

⁹When all the people* heard of Jesus' arrival, they flocked to see him and also to see Lazarus, the man Jesus had raised from the dead. ¹⁰Then the leading priests decided to kill Lazarus, too, ¹¹for it was because of him that many of the people had deserted them and believed in Jesus.

12:3 Greek *took 1 litra* [327 grams].   **12:5** Greek *300 denarii*. A denarius was equivalent to a full day's wage. **12:9** Greek *Jewish people;* also in 12:11.

11:48 The Jewish leaders knew that if they didn't stop Jesus, the Romans would discipline them. Rome gave partial freedom to the Jews as long as they were quiet and obedient. Jesus' miracles often caused a disturbance. The leaders feared that Rome's displeasure would bring additional hardship to their nation.

11:51 John regarded Caiaphas's statement as a prophecy. As high priest, Caiaphas was used by God to explain Jesus' death even though Caiaphas didn't realize what he was doing.

12:3 Essence of nard was a fragrant ointment imported from the mountains of India. Thus, it was very expensive. The amount Mary used was worth a year's wages.

12:4-6 Judas often dipped into the disciples' money bag for his own use. Quite likely, Jesus knew what Judas was doing (2:24, 25; 6:64), but never did or said anything about it. Similarly, when we choose the way of sin, God may not immediately do anything to stop us, but this does not mean he approves of our actions. What we deserve will come.

12:5, 6 Judas used a pious phrase to hide his true motives. But Jesus knew what was in his heart. Judas's life had become a lie, and the Devil was entering into him (13:27). Satan is the father of lies, and a lying character opens the door to his influence. Jesus' knowledge of us should make us want to keep our actions consistent with our words. Because we have nothing to fear with him, we should have nothing to hide.

12:7, 8 This act and Jesus' response to it do not teach us to ignore the poor so we can spend money extravagantly for Christ. This was a unique act for a specific occasion—an anointing that anticipated Jesus' burial and a public declaration of faith in him as Messiah. Jesus' words should have taught Judas a valuable lesson about the worth of money. Unfortunately, Judas did not take heed; soon he would sell his Master's life for 30 pieces of silver.

12:10, 11 The leading priests' blindness and hardness of heart caused them to sink ever deeper into sin. They rejected the Messiah and planned to kill him, and then plotted to murder Lazarus as well. One sin leads to another. From the Jewish leaders' point of view, they could accuse Jesus of blasphemy because he claimed equality with God. But Lazarus had done nothing of the kind. They wanted Lazarus dead simply because he was a living witness to Jesus' power. This is a warning to us to avoid sin. Sin leads to more sin, a downward spiral that can be stopped only by repentance and the power of the Holy Spirit to change our behavior.

Marginal references: 11:49 Matt 26:3 | 11:50 John 18:13-14 | 11:51 Exod 28:30; Num 27:21 | 11:52 Isa 49:6; John 10:16; 1 Jn 2:2 | 11:53 Matt 26:4 | 11:55 Exod 12:13; 2 Chr 30:17-19; Matt 26:1-2; Mark 14:1 | 12:1-8 //Matt 26:6-13; //Mark 14:3-9 | 12:1 John 11:1 | 12:2 Luke 10:38-42 | 12:3 Luke 7:37-38 | 12:4 John 6:71 | 12:6 John 13:29 | 12:7 John 19:40 | 12:8 Deut 15:11 | 12:10 Luke 16:31

Jesus Rides into Jerusalem on a Young Donkey
(**183**/Matthew 21:1-11; Mark 11:1-11; Luke 19:28-44)

12:12-19
//Matt 21:1-11
//Mark 11:1-11
//Luke 19:28-38

¹²The next day, the news that Jesus was on the way to Jerusalem swept through the city. A huge crowd of Passover visitors ¹³took palm branches and went down the road to meet him. They shouted,

12:13
Lev 23:40
†Ps 118:25-26
Zeph 3:15

"Praise God!*
Bless the one who comes in the name of the Lord!
Hail to the King of Israel!"*

¹⁴Jesus found a young donkey and sat on it, fulfilling the prophecy that said:

12:15
Isa 35:4
†Zech 9:9

¹⁵ "Don't be afraid, people of Israel.*
Look, your King is coming,
    sitting on a donkey's colt."*

¹⁶His disciples didn't realize at the time that this was a fulfillment of prophecy. But after Jesus entered into his glory, they remembered that these Scriptures had come true before their eyes.

12:16
John 2:22; 7:39

¹⁷Those in the crowd who had seen Jesus call Lazarus back to life were telling others all about it. ¹⁸That was the main reason so many went out to meet him—because they had heard about this mighty miracle. ¹⁹Then the Pharisees said to each other, "We've lost. Look, the whole world has gone after him!"

12:17
John 11:43-44

12:18
John 12:11; 19:37

Jesus Explains Why He Must Die (**185**)

12:21
John 1:43-44

²⁰Some Greeks who had come to Jerusalem to attend the Passover ²¹paid a visit to Philip, who was from Bethsaida in Galilee. They said, "Sir, we want to meet Jesus." ²²Philip told Andrew about it, and they went together to ask Jesus.

12:23
John 13:32; 17:1

12:24
1 Cor 15:36

²³Jesus replied, "The time has come for the Son of Man to enter into his glory. ²⁴The truth is, a kernel of wheat must be planted in the soil. Unless it dies it will be alone—a single seed. But its death will produce many new kernels—a plentiful harvest of new lives. ²⁵Those who love their life in this world will lose it. Those who despise their life in this world will keep it for eternal life. ²⁶All those who want to be my disciples must

12:25
Matt 10:39
Luke 9:24; 17:33

12:26
John 14:3; 17:24

12:13a Greek *Hosanna,* an exclamation of praise that literally means "save now."   **12:13b** Ps 118:25-26; Zeph 3:15.
12:15a Greek *daughter of Zion.*   **12:15b** Zech 9:9.

12:13 Jesus began his last week on earth by riding into Jerusalem on a donkey under a canopy of palm branches, with crowds hailing him as their king. To announce that he was indeed the Messiah, Jesus chose a *time* when all Israel would be gathered at Jerusalem, a *place* where huge crowds could see him, and a *way* of proclaiming his mission that was unmistakable. On Palm Sunday we celebrate Jesus' Triumphal Entry into Jerusalem.

12:13 The people who were praising God for giving them a king had the wrong idea about Jesus. They were sure he would be a national leader who would restore their nation to its former glory, and thus, they were deaf to the words of their prophets and blind to Jesus' real mission. When it became apparent that Jesus was not going to fulfill their hopes, many people turned against him.

12:16 After Jesus' resurrection, the disciples understood for the first time many of the prophecies that they had missed along the way. Jesus' words and actions took on new meaning and made more sense. In retrospect, the disciples saw how Jesus had led them into a deeper and better understanding of his truth. Stop now and think about the events in your life leading up to where you are now. How has God led you to this point? As you grow older, you will look back and see God's involvement more clearly than you do now.

12:18 The people flocked to Jesus because they had heard about his great miracle in raising Lazarus from the dead. Their adoration was short-lived and their commitment shallow, for in

a few days they would do nothing to stop his crucifixion. Devotion based only on curiosity or popularity fades quickly.

12:20, 21 These Greeks probably were converts to the Jewish faith. They may have gone to Philip because, though he was a Jew, he had a Greek name.

12:23-25 This is a beautiful picture of the necessary sacrifice of Jesus. Unless a kernel of wheat is planted in the soil, it will not become a blade of wheat producing many more seeds. Jesus had to die to pay the penalty for our sin, but also to show his power over death. His resurrection proves he has eternal life. Because Jesus is God, Jesus can give this same eternal life to all who believe in him.

12:25 We must be so committed to living for Christ that we "despise" our lives by comparison. This does not mean that we long to die or that we are careless or destructive with the life God has given, but that we are willing to die if doing so will glorify Christ. We must disown the tyrannical rule of our own self-centeredness. By laying aside our striving for advantage, security, and pleasure, we can serve God lovingly and freely. Releasing control of our lives and transferring control to Christ bring eternal life and genuine joy.

12:26 Many believed that Jesus came for the Jews only. But when Jesus said, "All those who want to be my disciples must come and follow me," he was talking to these Greeks as well. No matter who the sincere seekers are, Jesus welcomes them. His message is for everyone. Don't allow social or racial differences to become barriers to the Good News. Take the Good News to all people.

come and follow me, because my servants must be where I am. And if they follow me, the Father will honor them. ²⁷Now my soul is deeply troubled. Should I pray, 'Father, save me from what lies ahead'? But that is the very reason why I came! ²⁸Father, bring glory to your name."

Then a voice spoke from heaven, saying, "I have already brought it glory, and I will do it again." ²⁹When the crowd heard the voice, some thought it was thunder, while others declared an angel had spoken to him.

³⁰Then Jesus told them, "The voice was for your benefit, not mine. ³¹The time of judgment for the world has come, when the prince of this world* will be cast out.

12:31 *The prince of this world* is a name for Satan.

12:27
Ps 6:3
Matt 26:38
Mark 14:34

12:28
Matt 3:17; 17:5
Mark 1:11; 9:7
Luke 3:22; 9:35
2 Pet 1:17-18

12:31
John 14:30; 16:11
Eph 2:2

CAIAPHAS

Caiaphas was the leader of the religious group called the Sadducees. Educated and wealthy, they were politically influential in the nation. As the elite group, they were on fairly good terms with Rome. They hated Jesus because he endangered their secure life-styles and taught a message they could not accept. A kingdom in which leaders *served* had no appeal to them.

Caiaphas's usual policy was to remove any threats to his power by whatever means necessary. For Caiaphas, whether Jesus should die was not in question; the only point to be settled was *when* his death should take place. Not only did Jesus have to be captured and tried; the Jewish high council also needed Roman approval before they could carry out the death sentence. Caiaphas's plans were unexpectedly helped by Judas's offer to betray Christ.

Caiaphas did not realize that his schemes were actually part of a wonderful plan God was carrying out. Caiaphas's willingness to sacrifice another man to preserve his own security was decidedly selfish. By contrast, Jesus' willingness to die for us was a clear example of loving self-sacrifice. Caiaphas thought he had won the battle as Jesus hung on the cross, but he did not count on the Resurrection!

Caiaphas's mind was closed. He couldn't accept the Resurrection even when the evidence was overwhelming, and he attempted to silence those whose lives had been forever changed by the risen Christ (Matthew 28:12, 13). Caiaphas represents those people who will not believe because they think it will cost them too much to accept Jesus as Lord. They choose the fleeting power, prestige, and pleasures of this life instead of the eternal life God offers those who receive his Son. What is your choice?

Strength and accomplishment	• High priest for 18 years
Weaknesses and mistakes	• One of those most directly responsible for Jesus' death • Used his office as a means to power and personal security • Planned Jesus' capture, carried out his illegal trial, pressured Pilate to approve the Crucifixion, attempted to prevent the Resurrection, and later tried to cover up the fact of the Resurrection • Kept up religious appearances while compromising with Rome • Involved in the later persecution of Christians
Lessons from his life	• God uses even the twisted motives and actions of his enemies to bring about his will • When we cover selfish motives with spiritual objectives and words, God still sees our intentions
Vital statistics	• Where: Jerusalem • Occupation: High priest • Relative: Father-in-law: Annas • Contemporaries: Jesus, Pilate, Herod Antipas
Key verses	"And one of them, Caiaphas, who was high priest that year, said, 'How can you be so stupid? Why should the whole nation be destroyed? Let this one man die for the people' " (John 11:49, 50).

12:27 Jesus knew his crucifixion lay ahead, and because he was human, he dreaded it. He knew he would have to take the sins of the world on himself, and he knew this would separate him from his Father. He wanted to be delivered from this horrible death, but he knew that God sent him into the world to die for our sins, in our place. Jesus said no to his human desires in order to obey his Father and glorify him. Although we will never have to face such a difficult and awesome task, we are still called to obedience. Whatever the Father asks, we should do his will and bring glory to his name.

12:31 The prince of this world is Satan, an angel who rebelled against God. Satan is real, not symbolic, and is constantly working against God and those who obey him. Satan tempted Eve in the garden and persuaded her to sin; he tempted Jesus in the wilderness and did not persuade him to fall (Matthew 4:1-11). Satan has great power, but people can be delivered from his reign of spiritual darkness because of Christ's victory on the cross. Satan is powerful, but Jesus is much more powerful. Jesus' resurrection shattered Satan's deathly power (Colossians 1:13, 14). To overcome Satan we need faithful allegiance to God's Word, determination to stay away from sin, and the support of other believers.

32 And when I am lifted up on the cross,* I will draw everyone to myself." 33 He said this to indicate how he was going to die.

12:32
John 3:14; 6:44

34 "Die?" asked the crowd. "We understood from Scripture that the Messiah would live forever. Why are you saying the Son of Man will die? Who is this Son of Man you are talking about?"

12:34
Pss 89:4, 36; 110:4
Isa 9:7
Ezek 37:25
Dan 7:14

35 Jesus replied, "My light will shine out for you just a little while longer. Walk in it while you can, so you will not stumble when the darkness falls. If you walk in the darkness, you cannot see where you are going. 36 Believe in the light while there is still time; then you will become children of the light." After saying these things, Jesus went away and was hidden from them.

12:35
John 8:12; 9:4;
12:46

12:36
Luke 16:8
John 8:59
Eph 5:8
1 Thes 5:5

Most of the People Do Not Believe in Jesus (**186**)

37 But despite all the miraculous signs he had done, most of the people did not believe in him. 38 This is exactly what Isaiah the prophet had predicted:

12:38
†Isa 53:1
Rom 10:16

"Lord, who has believed our message?
　To whom will the Lord reveal his saving power?"*

39 But the people couldn't believe, for as Isaiah also said,

40 "The Lord has blinded their eyes
　　and hardened their hearts—
so their eyes cannot see,
　and their hearts cannot understand,
and they cannot turn to me
　and let me heal them."*

12:40
†Isa 6:10
Matt 13:14

41 Isaiah was referring to Jesus when he made this prediction, because he was given a vision of the Messiah's glory. 42 Many people, including some of the Jewish leaders, believed in him. But they wouldn't admit it to anyone because of their fear that the Pharisees would expel them from the synagogue. 43 For they loved human praise more than the praise of God.

12:41
Isa 6:1

12:42
John 7:13, 48;
9:22-23; 12:11

12:43
John 5:44

Jesus Summarizes His Message (**187**)

44 Jesus shouted to the crowds, "If you trust me, you are really trusting God who sent me. 45 For when you see me, you are seeing the one who sent me. 46 I have come as a light to

12:46
John 1:4; 3:19;
8:12; 9:5

12:32 Greek *lifted up from the earth.*   **12:38** Isa 53:1.   **12:40** Isa 6:10.

12:32-34 The crowd could not believe what Jesus was saying about the Messiah. They were waving palm branches for a victorious Messiah who would set up a political, earthly kingdom that would never end. From their reading of certain Scriptures, they thought the Messiah would never die (Psalms 89:35, 36; 110:4; Isaiah 9:7). Other passages, however, showed that he would die (Isaiah 53:5-9). Jesus' words did not mesh with their concept of the Messiah. First he had to suffer and die—then he would one day set up his eternal Kingdom. What kind of Messiah, or Savior, are you seeking? Beware of trying to force Jesus into your own mold—he won't fit.

12:35, 36 Jesus said he would be with them in person for only a short time, and they should take advantage of his presence while they had it. Like a light shining in a dark place, he would point out the way they should walk. If they walked in his light, they would become "children of the light," revealing the truth and pointing people to God. As Christians, we are to be Christ's light bearers, letting his light shine through us. How brightly is your light shining? Can others see Christ in your actions?

12:37, 38 Jesus had performed many miracles, but most people still didn't believe in him. Likewise, many today won't believe despite all God does. Don't be discouraged if your witness for Christ doesn't turn as many to him as you'd like. Your job is to continue as a faithful witness. You are responsible to reach out to others, but they are responsible for their own decisions.

12:39-41 People in Jesus' time, like those in the time of Isaiah, would not believe despite the evidence (12:37). As a result, God hardened their hearts. Does that mean God intentionally prevented these people from believing in him? No, he simply confirmed their own choices. After a lifetime of resisting God, they had become so set in their ways that they wouldn't even try to understand Jesus' message. For such people, it is virtually impossible to come to God—their hearts have been permanently hardened. Other instances of hardened hearts because of constant stubbornness are recorded in Exodus 9:12, Romans 1:24-28, and 2 Thessalonians 2:8-12.

12:42, 43 Along with those who refused to believe, many believed but refused to admit it. This is just as bad, and Jesus had strong words for such people (see Matthew 10:32, 33). People who will not take a stand for Jesus are afraid of rejection or ridicule. Many Jewish leaders wouldn't admit to faith in Jesus because they feared excommunication from the synagogue (which was their livelihood) and loss of their prestigious place in the community. But the praise of others is fickle and short-lived. We should be much more concerned about God's eternal acceptance than about the temporary approval of other people.

12:45 We often wonder what God is like. How can we know the Creator when he doesn't make himself visible? Jesus said plainly that those who see him see God, because he *is* God. If you want to know what God is like, study the person and words of Jesus Christ.

shine in this dark world, so that all who put their trust in me will no longer remain in the darkness. [47]If anyone hears me and doesn't obey me, I am not his judge—for I have come to save the world and not to judge it. [48]But all who reject me and my message will be judged at the day of judgment by the truth I have spoken. [49]I don't speak on my own authority. The Father who sent me gave me his own instructions as to what I should say. [50]And I know his instructions lead to eternal life; so I say whatever the Father tells me to say!"

12:47
John 3:17; 8:15

C. DEATH AND RESURRECTION OF JESUS, THE SON OF GOD (13:1—21:25)

John begins his Gospel with eternity and ends with Jesus coming to earth again. He features Jesus teaching his disciples privately just before his arrest and death. We see, clearly, the deep love Jesus has for the believer and the peace that comes from faith. Knowing the love Jesus has for believers, we, too, should believe and allow Jesus to forgive our sins. Only then will we experience peace in a world filled with turmoil.

1. Jesus teaches his disciples

Jesus Washes the Disciples' Feet (**210**)

13 Before the Passover celebration, Jesus knew that his hour had come to leave this world and return to his Father. He now showed the disciples the full extent of his love.* [2]It was time for supper, and the Devil had already enticed Judas, son of Simon Iscariot, to carry out his plan to betray Jesus. [3]Jesus knew that the Father had given him authority over everything and that he had come from God and would return to God. [4]So he got up from the table, took off his robe, wrapped a towel around his waist, [5]and poured water into a basin. Then he began to wash the disciples' feet and to wipe them with the towel he had around him.

[6]When he came to Simon Peter, Peter said to him, "Lord, why are you going to wash my feet?"

[7]Jesus replied, "You don't understand now why I am doing it; someday you will."

[8]"No," Peter protested, "you will never wash my feet!"

Jesus replied, "But if I don't wash you, you won't belong to me."

[9]Simon Peter exclaimed, "Then wash my hands and head as well, Lord, not just my feet!"

[10]Jesus replied, "A person who has bathed all over does not need to wash, except for the feet,* to be entirely clean. And you are clean, but that isn't true of everyone here."

13:1
John 16:28; 17:1

13:2
Luke 22:3
John 6:70-71

13:4
Luke 12:37; 22:27

13:5
Luke 7:44
John 12:3

13:8
Ezek 36:25
1 Cor 6:11
Eph 5:26
Titus 3:5

13:10
John 15:3

13:1 Or *He loved his disciples to the very end.* **13:10** Some manuscripts do not include *except for the feet.*

12:48 The purpose of Jesus' first mission on earth was not to judge people, but to show them the way to find salvation and eternal life. When he comes again, one of his main purposes will be to judge people for how they lived on earth. Christ's words that we would *not* accept and obey will condemn us. On the day of judgment, those who accepted Jesus and lived his way will be raised to eternal life (1 Corinthians 15:51-57; 1 Thessalonians 4:15-18; Revelation 21:1-7), and those who rejected Jesus and lived any way they pleased will face eternal punishment (Revelation 20:11-15). Decide now which side you'll be on, for the consequences of your decision last forever.

13:1 Jesus knew he would be betrayed by one of his disciples, denied by another, and deserted by all of them for a time. Still he "now showed the disciples the full extent of his love." God knows us completely, as Jesus knew his disciples (2:24, 25; 6:64). He knows the sins we have committed and the ones we will yet commit. Still, he loves us. How do you respond to that kind of love?

13:1ff Chapters 13–17 tell us what Jesus said to his disciples on the night before his death. These words were all spoken in one evening when, with only the disciples as his audience, he gave final instructions to prepare them for his death and resurrection, events that would change their lives forever.

13:1-3 For more information on Judas Iscariot, see his Profile in Mark 14.

13:1-17 Jesus was the model servant, and he showed his servant attitude to his disciples. Washing guests' feet was a job for a household servant to carry out when guests arrived. But Jesus wrapped a towel around his waist, as the lowliest slave would do, and washed and dried his disciples' feet. If even he, God in the flesh, is willing to serve, we his followers must also be servants, willing to serve in any way that glorifies God. Are you willing to follow Christ's example of serving? Whom can you serve today? There is a special blessing for those who not only agree that humble service is Christ's way, but who also follow through and do it (13:17).

13:6, 7 Imagine being Peter and watching Jesus wash the others' feet, all the while moving closer to you. Seeing his Master behave like a slave must have confused Peter. He still did not understand Jesus' teaching that to be a leader, a person must be a servant. This is not a comfortable passage for leaders who find it hard to serve those beneath them. How do you treat those who work under you (whether children, employees, or volunteers)?

[11] For Jesus knew who would betray him. That is what he meant when he said, "Not all of you are clean."

[12] After washing their feet, he put on his robe again and sat down and asked, "Do you understand what I was doing? [13] You call me 'Teacher' and 'Lord,' and you are right, because it is true. [14] And since I, the Lord and Teacher, have washed your feet, you ought to wash each other's feet. [15] I have given you an example to follow. Do as I have done to you. [16] How true it is that a servant is not greater than the master. Nor are messengers more important than the one who sends them. [17] You know these things—now do them! That is the path of blessing.

[18] "I am not saying these things to all of you; I know so well each one of you I chose. The Scriptures declare, 'The one who shares my food has turned against me,'* and this will soon come true. [19] I tell you this now, so that when it happens you will believe I am the Messiah. [20] Truly, anyone who welcomes my messenger is welcoming me, and anyone who welcomes me is welcoming the Father who sent me."

13:11
John 6:64, 70-71; 13:2

13:13
1 Cor 12:3

13:14
Luke 22:27
1 Tim 5:10
1 Pet 5:5

13:15
Phil 2:5-7
1 Pet 5:3-5
1 Jn 2:6; 3:16

13:17
Jas 1:25

13:18
†Ps 41:9

13:20
Matt 10:40
Luke 10:16

Jesus and the Disciples Share the Last Supper
(**211**/Matthew 26:20-30; Mark 14:17-26; Luke 22:14-30)

[21] Now Jesus was in great anguish of spirit, and he exclaimed, "The truth is, one of you will betray me!"

[22] The disciples looked at each other, wondering whom he could mean. [23] One of Jesus' disciples, the one Jesus loved, was sitting next to Jesus at the table.* [24] Simon Peter motioned to him to ask who would do this terrible thing. [25] Leaning toward Jesus, he asked, "Lord, who is it?"

[26] Jesus said, "It is the one to whom I give the bread dipped in the sauce." And when he had dipped it, he gave it to Judas, son of Simon Iscariot. [27] As soon as Judas had eaten the bread, Satan entered into him. Then Jesus told him, "Hurry. Do it now." [28] None of the others at the table knew what Jesus meant. [29] Since Judas was their treasurer, some thought Jesus was telling him to go and pay for the food or to give some money to the poor. [30] So Judas left at once, going out into the night.

13:21-30
//Matt 26:21-25
//Mark 14:18-21
//Luke 22:21-23

13:23
John 19:26

13:25
John 21:20

13:27
Luke 22:3
John 13:2

13:29
John 12:6

13:30
Luke 22:53

Jesus Predicts Peter's Denial (**212**/Luke 22:31-38)

[31] As soon as Judas left the room, Jesus said, "The time has come for me, the Son of Man, to enter into my glory, and God will receive glory because of all that happens to me. [32] And God will bring* me into my glory very soon. [33] Dear children, how brief are these moments before I must go away and leave you! Then, though you search for me, you cannot come to me—just as I told the Jewish leaders. [34] So now I am giving you a new commandment: Love each other. Just as I have loved you, you should love each other. [35] Your love for one another will prove to the world that you are my disciples."

13:34
Lev 19:18
Eph 5:2
1 Thes 4:9
1 Pet 1:22
1 Jn 2:8; 3:23; 4:10-11

13:35
1 Jn 3:14; 4:20

13:18 Ps 41:9.   **13:23** Greek *was reclining on Jesus' bosom.* The "disciple whom Jesus loved" was probably John.
13:32 Some manuscripts read *And if God is glorified in him [the Son of Man], God will bring.*

13:12ff Jesus did not wash his disciples' feet just to get them to be nice to each other. His far greater goal was to extend his mission on earth after he was gone. These men were to move into the world serving God, serving each other, and serving all people to whom they took the message of salvation.

13:22 Judas was not the obvious betrayer. After all, he was the one the disciples trusted to keep the money (12:6; 13:29).

13:26 The honored guest at a meal was often singled out like this.

13:27 Satan's part in the betrayal of Jesus does not remove any of the responsibility from Judas. Disillusioned because Jesus was talking about dying rather than setting up his Kingdom, Judas may have been trying to force Jesus' hand and make him use his power to prove he was the Messiah. Or perhaps Judas, not understanding Jesus' mission, no longer believed Jesus was God's chosen one. Whatever Judas thought, Satan assumed that Jesus' death would end his mission and thwart God's plan. Like Judas, Satan did not know that Jesus' death was the most important part of God's plan all along.

13:27-38 John describes these few moments in clear detail. We can see that Jesus knew exactly what was going to happen. He

knew about Judas and about Peter, but he did not change the situation, nor did he stop loving them. In the same way, Jesus knows exactly what you will do to hurt him. Yet he still loves you unconditionally and will forgive you whenever you ask him. Judas couldn't understand this, and his life ended tragically. Peter understood, and despite his shortcomings, his life ended triumphantly because he never let go of his faith in the one who loved him.

13:34 To love others was not a new commandment (see Leviticus 19:18), but to love others as much as Christ loved others was revolutionary. Now we are to love others based on Jesus' sacrificial love for us. Such love will not only bring unbelievers to Christ; it will also keep believers strong and united in a world hostile to God. Jesus was a living example of God's love, as we are to be living examples of Jesus' love.

13:34, 35 Jesus says that our Christlike love will show we are his disciples. Do people see petty bickering, jealousy, and division in your church? Or do they know you are Jesus' followers by your love for one another?

13:35 Love is more than simply warm feelings; it is an attitude that reveals itself in action. How can we love others as Jesus loves

13:36-38
//Matt 26:33-35
//Mark 14:29-31
//Luke 22:33-34

13:36
John 21:18
2 Pet 1:14

14:2
Ps 90:1
John 2:16, 19-21;

14:3
John 14:10-11,
18-20; 16:16-22

³⁶Simon Peter said, "Lord, where are you going?"

And Jesus replied, "You can't go with me now, but you will follow me later."

³⁷"But why can't I come now, Lord?" he asked. "I am ready to die for you."

³⁸Jesus answered, "Die for me? No, before the rooster crows tomorrow morning, you will deny three times that you even know me.

Jesus Is the Way to the Father (**213**)

14 "Don't be troubled. You trust God, now trust in me. ²There are many rooms in my Father's home, and I am going to prepare a place for you. If this were not so, I would tell you plainly. ³When everything is ready, I will come and get you, so

Being loved is the most powerful motivation in the world! Our ability to love is often shaped by our experience of love. We usually love others as we have been loved.

Some of the greatest statements about God's loving nature were written by a man who experienced God's love in a unique way. John, Jesus' disciple, expressed his relationship to the Son of God by calling himself "the disciple Jesus loved" (21:20). Although Jesus' love is clearly communicated in all the Gospels, in John's Gospel it is a central theme. Because his own experience of Jesus' love was so strong and personal, John was sensitive to those words and actions of Jesus that illustrated how the one who *is* love loved others.

Jesus knew John fully and loved him fully. He gave John and his brother James the nickname "Sons of Thunder," perhaps from an occasion when the brothers asked Jesus for permission to "order down fire from heaven" (Luke 9:54) on a village that had refused to welcome Jesus and the disciples. In John's Gospel and letters, we see the great God of love, while the thunder of God's justice bursts from the pages of Revelation.

Jesus confronts each of us as he confronted John. We cannot know the depth of Jesus' love unless we are willing to face the fact that he knows us completely. Otherwise we are fooled into believing he must love the people we pretend to be, not the sinners we actually are. John and all the disciples convince us that God is able and willing to accept us as we are. Being aware of God's love is a great motivator for change. His love is not given in exchange for our efforts; his love frees us to really live. Have you accepted that love?

Strengths and accomplishments	• Before following Jesus, was one of John the Baptist's disciples • One of the 12 disciples and, with Peter and James, one of the inner three, closest to Jesus • Wrote five New Testament books: the Gospel of John; 1, 2, and 3 John; and Revelation
Weaknesses and mistakes	• Along with James, shared a tendency to outbursts of selfishness and anger • Asked for a special position in Jesus' Kingdom
Lessons from his life	• Those who realize how much they are loved are able to love much • When God changes a life, he does not take away personality characteristics, but puts them to effective use in his service
Vital statistics	• Occupations: Fisherman, disciple • Relatives: Father: Zebedee. Mother: Salome. Brother: James • Contemporaries: Jesus, Pilate, Herod
Key verses	"Dear friends, I am not writing a new commandment, for it is an old one you have always had, right from the beginning. This commandment—to love one another—is the same message you heard before. Yet it is also new. This commandment is true in Christ and is true among you, because the darkness is disappearing and the true light is already shining" (1 John 2:7, 8).

John's story is told throughout the Gospels, Acts, and Revelation.

us? By helping when it's not convenient, by giving when it hurts, by devoting energy to others' welfare rather than our own, by absorbing hurts from others without complaining or fighting back. This kind of loving is hard to do. That is why people notice when you do it and know you are empowered by a supernatural source. The Bible has another beautiful description of love in 1 Corinthians 13.

13:37, 38 Peter proudly told Jesus that he was ready to die for him. But Jesus corrected him. He knew Peter would deny that he knew Jesus that very night to protect himself (18:15-18, 25-27). In our enthusiasm, it is easy to make promises, but God knows the extent of our commitment. Paul tells us not to think of ourselves more highly than we ought (Romans 12:3). Instead of bragging, demonstrate your commitment step by

step as you grow in your knowledge of God's Word and in your faith.

14:1-3 Jesus' words show that the way to eternal life, though unseen, is secure—as secure as your trust in Jesus. He has already prepared the way to eternal life. The only issue that may still be unsettled is your willingness to believe.

14:2, 3 There are few verses in Scripture that describe eternal life, but these few verses are rich with promises. Here Jesus says, "I am going to prepare a place for you," and "I will come and get you." We can look forward to eternal life because Jesus has promised it to all who believe in him. Although the details of eternity are unknown, we need not fear because Jesus is preparing for us and will spend eternity with us.

that you will always be with me where I am. ⁴And you know where I am going and how to get there."

⁵"No, we don't know, Lord," Thomas said. "We haven't any idea where you are going, so how can we know the way?"

⁶Jesus told him, "I am the way, the truth, and the life. No one can come to the Father except through me. ⁷If you had known who I am, then you would have known who my Father is.* From now on you know him and have seen him!"

⁸Philip said, "Lord, show us the Father and we will be satisfied."

⁹Jesus replied, "Philip, don't you even yet know who I am, even after all the time I have been with you? Anyone who has seen me has seen the Father! So why are you asking to see him? ¹⁰Don't you believe that I am in the Father and the Father is in me? The words I say are not my own, but my Father who lives in me does his work through me. ¹¹Just believe that I am in the Father and the Father is in me. Or at least believe because of what you have seen me do.

¹²"The truth is, anyone who believes in me will do the same works I have done, and even greater works, because I am going to be with the Father. ¹³You can ask for anything in my name, and I will do it, because the work of the Son brings glory to the Father. ¹⁴Yes, ask anything in my name, and I will do it!

Jesus Promises the Holy Spirit (214)

¹⁵"If you love me, obey my commandments. ¹⁶And I will ask the Father, and he will give you another Counselor,* who will never leave you. ¹⁷He is the Holy Spirit, who leads into all truth. The world at large cannot receive him, because it isn't looking for him and doesn't recognize him. But you do, because he lives with you now and later will be in you. ¹⁸No, I will not abandon you as orphans—I will come to you. ¹⁹In just a little

14:6
John 1:4, 14, 16;
8:32; 10:10; 11:25
Rom 5:2
Eph 2:18
Heb 10:20
1 Jn 5:20

14:7
John 6:46; 8:19
1 Jn 2:13

14:9
John 1:14, 18;
12:45
2 Cor 4:4
Col 1:15
Heb 1:3

14:10
John 5:19; 10:38;
17:11, 21-24

14:16
John 14:26; 15:26

14:17
Rom 8:15-16
1 Jn 3:24

14:18
Rom 8:9-11
2 Cor 3:17-18

14:7 Some manuscripts read *If you really have known me, you will know who my Father is.*   **14:16** Or *Comforter,* or *Encourager,* or *Advocate.* Greek *Paraclete;* also in 14:26.

14:5, 6 This is one of the most basic and important passages in Scripture. How can we know the way to God? Only through Jesus. Jesus is the way because he is both God and man. By uniting our lives with his, we are united with God. Trust Jesus to take you to the Father, and all the benefits of being God's child will be yours.

14:6 Jesus says he is the *only* way to God the Father. Some people may argue that this way is too narrow. In reality, it is wide enough for the whole world, if the world chooses to accept it. Instead of worrying about how limited it sounds to have only one way, we should be saying, "Thank you, God, for providing a sure way to get to you!"

14:6 As the *way,* Jesus is our path to the Father. As the *truth,* he is the reality of all God's promises. As the *life,* he joins his divine life to ours, both now and eternally.

14:9 Jesus is the visible, tangible image of the invisible God. He is the complete revelation of what God is like. Jesus explained to Philip, who wanted to see the Father, that to know Jesus is to know God. The search for God, for truth and reality, ends in Christ. (See also Colossians 1:15; Hebrews 1:1-4.)

14:12, 13 Jesus is not saying that his disciples would do greater works—after all, raising the dead is about as amazing as you can get. Rather, the disciples, working in the power of the Holy Spirit, would carry the Good News of God's Kingdom out of Palestine and into the whole world.

14:14 When Jesus says we can ask for anything, we must remember that our asking must be in his name—that is, according to God's character and will. God will not grant requests contrary to his nature or his will, and we cannot use his name as a magic formula to fulfill our selfish desires. If we are sincerely following God and seeking to do his will, then our requests will be in line with what he wants, and he will grant them. (See also 15:16; 16:23.)

14:15, 16 Jesus was soon going to leave the disciples, but he would remain with them. How could this be? The Counselor—the

Spirit of God himself—would come after Jesus was gone to care for and guide the disciples. The regenerating power of the Spirit came on the disciples just before Jesus' ascension (20:22), and the Spirit was poured out on all the believers at Pentecost (Acts 2), shortly after Jesus ascended to heaven. The Holy Spirit is the very presence of God within us and all believers, helping us live as God wants and building Christ's church on earth. By faith we can appropriate the Spirit's power each day.

14:16 The word translated "Counselor" combines the ideas of comfort and counsel (see NLT text note). The Holy Spirit is a powerful person on our side, working for and with us.

14:17ff The following chapters teach these truths about the Holy Spirit: He will never leave us (14:16); the world at large cannot receive him (14:17); he lives with us and in us (14:17); he teaches us (14:26); he reminds us of Jesus' words (14:26; 15:26); he convinces us of sin, shows us God's righteousness, and announces God's judgment on evil (16:8); he guides into truth and gives insight into future events (16:13); he brings glory to Christ (16:14). The Holy Spirit has been active among people from the beginning of time, but after Pentecost (Acts 2) he came to live in all believers. Many people are unaware of the Holy Spirit's activities, but to those who hear Christ's words and understand the Spirit's power, the Spirit gives a whole new way to look at life.

14:18 When Jesus said, "I will come to you," he meant it. Although Jesus ascended to heaven, he sent the Holy Spirit to live in believers, and to have the Holy Spirit is to have Jesus himself.

14:19-21 Sometimes people wish they knew the future so they could prepare for it. God has chosen not to give us this knowledge. He alone knows what will happen, but he tells us all we need to know to *prepare* for the future. When we live by his standards, he will not leave us; he will come to us, he will be in us, and he will show himself to us. God knows what will happen, and because he will be with us through it all, we need not fear. We don't have to know the future to have faith in God; we have to have faith in God to be secure about the future.

14:20
John 10:38; 15:4-5;
16:16, 23; 17:21-24

14:21
John 15:10; 16:27
1 Jn 2:5
2 Jn 1:6

14:22
Luke 6:16
Acts 10:41

14:23
Ps 91:1
John 15:10
Eph 3:17
1 Jn 4:16; 5:3
Rev 3:20; 21:3

14:24
John 7:16; 14:10

14:26
John 1:33; 15:26;
16:7; 20:22
1 Jn 2:20, 27

14:27
John 16:33; 20:19
Phil 4:7
Col 3:15

14:29
John 13:19

14:30
John 12:31

14:31
John 10:18; 12:49

while the world will not see me again, but you will. For I will live again, and you will, too. ²⁰When I am raised to life again, you will know that I am in my Father, and you are in me, and I am in you. ²¹Those who obey my commandments are the ones who love me. And because they love me, my Father will love them, and I will love them. And I will reveal myself to each one of them."

²²Judas (not Judas Iscariot, but the other disciple with that name) said to him, "Lord, why are you going to reveal yourself only to us and not to the world at large?"

²³Jesus replied, "All those who love me will do what I say. My Father will love them, and we will come to them and live with them. ²⁴Anyone who doesn't love me will not do what I say. And remember, my words are not my own. This message is from the Father who sent me. ²⁵I am telling you these things now while I am still with you. ²⁶But when the Father sends the Counselor as my representative—and by the Counselor I mean the Holy Spirit—he will teach you everything and will remind you of everything I myself have told you.

²⁷"I am leaving you with a gift—peace of mind and heart. And the peace I give isn't like the peace the world gives. So don't be troubled or afraid. ²⁸Remember what I told you: I am going away, but I will come back to you again. If you really love me, you will be very happy for me, because now I can go to the Father, who is greater than I am. ²⁹I have told you these things before they happen so that you will believe when they do happen.

³⁰"I don't have much more time to talk to you, because the prince of this world approaches. He has no power over me, ³¹but I will do what the Father requires of me, so that the world will know that I love the Father. Come, let's be going.

Jesus Teaches about the Vine and the Branches (**215**)

15 "I am the true vine, and my Father is the gardener. ²He cuts off every branch that doesn't produce fruit, and he prunes the branches that do bear fruit so they will produce even more. ³You have already been pruned for greater fruitfulness by the

15:3
John 17:17
Eph 5:26

14:21 Jesus said that his followers show their love for him by obeying him. Love is more than lovely words; it is commitment and conduct. If you love Christ, then prove it by obeying what he says in his Word.

14:22, 23 Because the disciples were still expecting Jesus to establish an earthly kingdom and overthrow Rome, they found it hard to understand why he did not tell the world at large that he was the Messiah. Not everyone, however, could understand Jesus' message. Ever since Pentecost, the Good News of the Kingdom has been proclaimed in the whole world, and yet not everyone is receptive to it. Jesus saves the deepest revelations of himself for those who love and obey him.

14:26 Jesus promised the disciples that the Holy Spirit would help them remember what he had been teaching them. This promise ensures the validity of the New Testament. The disciples were eyewitnesses of Jesus' life and teachings, and the Holy Spirit helped them remember without taking away their individual perspectives. We can be confident that the Gospels are accurate records of what Jesus taught and did (see 1 Corinthians 2:10-14). The Holy Spirit can help us in the same way. As we study the Bible, we can trust him to plant truth in our mind, convince us of God's will, and remind us when we stray from it.

14:27 The end result of the Holy Spirit's work in our lives is deep and lasting peace. Unlike worldly peace, which is usually defined as the absence of conflict, this peace is confident assurance in any circumstance; with Christ's peace, we have no need to fear the present or the future. If your life is full of stress, allow the Holy Spirit to fill you with Christ's peace (see Philippians 4:6, 7 for more on experiencing God's peace).

14:27-29 Sin, fear, uncertainty, doubt, and numerous other forces are at war within us. The peace of God moves into our hearts and lives to restrain these hostile forces and offer comfort in place of conflict. Jesus says he will give us that peace if we are willing to accept it from him.

14:28 As God the Son, Jesus willingly submits to God the Father. On earth, Jesus also submitted to many of the physical limitations of his humanity (Philippians 2:6).

14:30, 31 Although Satan, the prince of this world, was unable to overpower Jesus (Matthew 4), he still had the arrogance to try. Satan's power exists only because God allows him to act. But because Jesus is sinless, Satan has no power over him. If we obey Jesus and align ourselves closely with God's purposes, Satan can have no power over us.

14:31 "Come, let's be going" suggests that chapters 15–17 may have been spoken en route to the Garden of Gethsemane. Another view is that Jesus was asking the disciples to get ready to leave the upper room, but they did not actually do so until 18:1.

15:1 The grapevine is a prolific plant; a single vine bears many grapes. In the Old Testament, grapes symbolized Israel's fruitfulness in doing God's work on the earth (Psalm 80:8; Isaiah 5:1-7; Ezekiel 19:10-14). In the Passover meal, the fruit of the vine symbolized God's goodness to his people.

15:1ff Christ is the vine, and God is the gardener who cares for the branches to make them fruitful. The branches are all those who claim to be followers of Christ. The fruitful branches are true believers who by their living union with Christ produce much fruit. But those who become unproductive—those who turn back from following Christ after making a superficial commitment—will be separated from the vine. Unproductive followers are as good as dead and will be cut off and tossed aside.

15:2, 3 Jesus makes a distinction between two kinds of pruning: (1) cutting off and (2) cutting back branches. Fruitful branches are cut back to promote growth. In other words, God must sometimes discipline us to strengthen our character and faith. But branches that don't bear fruit are cut off at the trunk not only because they are worthless but also because they often infect the rest of the tree. People who don't bear fruit for God or who try to block the efforts of God's followers will be cut off from his life-giving power.

message I have given you. ⁴Remain in me, and I will remain in you. For a branch cannot produce fruit if it is severed from the vine, and you cannot be fruitful apart from me.

⁵"Yes, I am the vine; you are the branches. Those who remain in me, and I in them, will produce much fruit. For apart from me you can do nothing. ⁶Anyone who parts from me is thrown away like a useless branch and withers. Such branches are gathered into a pile to be burned. ⁷But if you stay joined to me and my words remain in you, you may ask any request you like, and it will be granted! ⁸My true disciples produce much fruit. This brings great glory to my Father.

⁹"I have loved you even as the Father has loved me. Remain in my love. ¹⁰When you obey me, you remain in my love, just as I obey my Father and remain in his love. ¹¹I have told you this so that you will be filled with my joy. Yes, your joy will overflow! ¹²I command you to love each other in the same way that I love you. ¹³And here is how to measure it—the greatest love is shown when people lay down their lives for their friends. ¹⁴You are my friends if you obey me. ¹⁵I no longer call you servants, because a master doesn't confide in his servants. Now you are my friends, since I have told you everything the Father told me. ¹⁶You didn't choose me. I chose you. I appointed you to go and produce fruit that will last, so that the Father will give you whatever you ask for, using my name. ¹⁷I command you to love each other.

Jesus Warns about the World's Hatred (216)

¹⁸"When the world hates you, remember it hated me before it hated you. ¹⁹The world would love you if you belonged to it, but you don't. I chose you to come out of the world, and so it hates you. ²⁰Do you remember what I told you? 'A servant is not greater than the master.' Since they persecuted me, naturally they will persecute you. And if they had listened to me, they would listen to you! ²¹The people of the world will hate you because you belong to me, for they don't know God who sent me. ²²They would not be guilty if I had not come and spoken to them. But now they have no excuse for their sin. ²³Anyone who hates me hates my Father, too. ²⁴If I hadn't done such miraculous signs among them that no one else could do, they would not be counted guilty. But as it is, they saw all that I did and yet hated both of us—me and my Father. ²⁵This has fulfilled what the Scriptures said: 'They hated me without cause.'*

15:25 Pss 35:19; 69:4.

15:4
John 6:56

15:6
Matt 3:10; 7:19; 13:42

15:8
Matt 5:16

15:9
John 3:35

15:10
John 14:15

15:11
John 17:13
1 Jn 1:4

15:12
John 13:34

15:13
John 10:11
Rom 5:6-8

15:16
Rom 1:13
Phil 1:22

15:18
John 7:7
1 Jn 3:13

15:19
John 17:14
1 Jn 4:5

15:21
Matt 5:11
1 Pet 4:14

15:22
John 9:41

15:24
John 5:36; 9:41

15:25
†Pss 35:19; 69:4

15:5 "Fruit" is not limited to soul winning. In this chapter, answered prayer, joy, and love are mentioned as fruit (15:7, 11, 12). Galatians 5:22-24 and 2 Peter 1:5-8 describe additional fruit: qualities of Christian character.

15:5, 6 Remaining in Christ means (1) believing that he is God's Son (1 John 4:15), (2) receiving him as Savior and Lord (John 1:12), (3) doing what God says (1 John 3:24), (4) continuing to believe the Good News (1 John 2:24), and (5) relating in love to the community of believers, Christ's body (John 15:12).

15:5-8 Many people try to be good, honest people who do what is right. But Jesus says that the only way to live a truly good life is to stay close to him, like a branch attached to the vine. Apart from Christ our efforts are unfruitful. Are you receiving the nourishment and life offered by Christ, the vine? If not, you are missing a special gift he has for you.

15:8 When a vine produces "much fruit," God is glorified, for daily he sent the sunshine and rain to make the crops grow, and constantly he nurtured each tiny plant and prepared it to blossom. What a moment of glory for the Lord of the harvest when the harvest is brought into the barns, mature and ready for use! He made it all happen! This farming analogy shows how God is glorified when people come into a right relationship with him and begin to "produce much fruit" in their lives.

15:11 When things are going well, we feel elated. When hardships come, we sink into depression. But true joy transcends the rolling waves of circumstance. Joy comes from a consistent relationship with Jesus Christ. When our lives are intertwined with his, he will help us walk through adversity without sinking into debilitating lows and manage prosperity without moving into deceptive highs. The joy of living with Jesus Christ daily will keep us levelheaded, no matter how high or low our circumstances.

15:12, 13 We are to love each other as Jesus loved us, and he loved us enough to give his life for us. We may not have to die for someone, but there are other ways to practice sacrificial love: listening, helping, encouraging, giving. Think of someone in particular who needs this kind of love today. Give all the love you can, and then try to give a little more.

15:15 Because Jesus Christ is Lord and Master, he should call us servants; instead, he calls us friends. How comforting and reassuring to be chosen as Christ's friends. Because he is Lord and Master, we owe him our unqualified obedience, but most of all, Jesus asks us to obey him because we love him.

15:16 Jesus made the first choice—to love and to die for us, to invite us to live with him forever. We make the next choice—to accept or reject his offer. Without *his* choice, we would have no choice to make.

15:17 Christians will get plenty of hatred from the world; from each other we need love and support. Do you allow small problems to get in the way of loving other believers? Jesus commands that you love them, and he will give you the strength to do it.

15:26
John 14:17
1 Jn 5:7

15:27
John 21:24
1 Jn 1:2; 4:14

16:2
John 9:22

16:3
John 15:21

16:4
John 13:19

16:5
John 7:33; 13:36

16:7
John 14:26; 15:26

16:9
John 15:22

16:10
Acts 3:14; 7:52
Rom 1:17
1 Pet 3:18

16:11
John 12:31

16:13
John 14:17, 26

16:15
John 17:10

16:16
John 14:18-24

26 "But I will send you the Counselor*—the Spirit of truth. He will come to you from the Father and will tell you all about me. 27 And you must also tell others about me because you have been with me from the beginning.

16 "I have told you these things so that you won't fall away. 2 For you will be expelled from the synagogues, and the time is coming when those who kill you will think they are doing God a service. 3 This is because they have never known the Father or me. 4 Yes, I'm telling you these things now, so that when they happen, you will remember I warned you. I didn't tell you earlier because I was going to be with you for a while longer.

Jesus Teaches about the Holy Spirit (217)

5 "But now I am going away to the one who sent me, and none of you has asked me where I am going. 6 Instead, you are very sad. 7 But it is actually best for you that I go away, because if I don't, the Counselor* won't come. If I do go away, he will come because I will send him to you. 8 And when he comes, he will convince the world of its sin, and of God's righteousness, and of the coming judgment. 9 The world's sin is unbelief in me. 10 Righteousness is available because I go to the Father, and you will see me no more. 11 Judgment will come because the prince of this world has already been judged.

12 "Oh, there is so much more I want to tell you, but you can't bear it now. 13 When the Spirit of truth comes, he will guide you into all truth. He will not be presenting his own ideas; he will be telling you what he has heard. He will tell you about the future. 14 He will bring me glory by revealing to you whatever he receives from me. 15 All that the Father has is mine; this is what I mean when I say that the Spirit will reveal to you whatever he receives from me.

Jesus Teaches about Using His Name in Prayer (218)

16 "In just a little while I will be gone, and you won't see me anymore. Then, just a little while after that, you will see me again."

17 The disciples asked each other, "What does he mean when he says, 'You won't see me, and then you will see me'? And what does he mean when he says, 'I am going to the Father'? 18 And what does he mean by 'a little while'? We don't understand."

15:26 Or *Comforter,* or *Encourager,* or *Advocate.* Greek *Paraclete.*   **16:7** Or *Comforter,* or *Encourager,* or *Advocate.* Greek *Paraclete.*

15:26 Once again Jesus offers hope. The Holy Spirit gives strength to endure the unreasonable hatred and evil in our world and the hostility many have toward Christ. This is especially comforting for those facing persecution.

15:26 Jesus uses two names for the Holy Spirit—"Counselor" and "Spirit of truth." The word *Counselor* conveys the helping, encouraging, and strengthening work of the Spirit. *Spirit of truth* points to the teaching, illuminating, and reminding work of the Spirit. The Holy Spirit ministers to both the head and the heart, and both dimensions are important.

16:1-16 In his last moments with his disciples, Jesus (1) warned them about further persecution, (2) told them where, when, and why he was going, and (3) assured them that they would not be left alone, but that the Spirit would come. Jesus knew what lay ahead, and he did not want the disciples' faith shaken or destroyed. God wants you to know you are not alone. You have the Holy Spirit to comfort you, teach you truth, and help you.

16:2 Saul (who later became Paul), under the authority of the high priest, went through the land hunting down and persecuting Christians, convinced that he was doing the right thing (Acts 9:1, 2; 26:9-11).

16:5 Although the disciples had asked Jesus about his death (13:36; 14:5), they had never wondered about its meaning. They were mostly concerned about themselves. If Jesus went away, what would become of them?

16:7 Unless Jesus did what he came to do, there would be no Good News. If he did not die, he could not remove our sins; he could not rise again and defeat death. If he did not go back to the Father, the Holy Spirit would not come. Christ's presence on earth was limited to one place at a time. His leaving meant he could be present to the whole world through the Holy Spirit.

16:8-11 Three important tasks of the Holy Spirit are (1) convincing the world of its sin and calling it to repentance, (2) revealing the standard of God's righteousness to anyone who believes, because Christ would no longer be physically present on earth, and (3) demonstrating Christ's judgment over Satan.

16:9 According to Jesus, not believing in him is *sin.*

16:10, 11 Christ's death on the cross made a personal relationship with God available to us. When we confess our sin, God declares us righteous and delivers us from judgment for our sins.

16:13 The truth into which the Holy Spirit guides us is the truth about Christ. The Spirit also helps us through patient practice to discern right from wrong.

16:13 Jesus said the Holy Spirit would tell them "about the future"—the nature of their mission, the opposition they would face, and the final outcome of their efforts. They didn't fully understand these promises until the Holy Spirit came after Jesus' death and resurrection. Then the Holy Spirit revealed truths to the disciples that they wrote down in the books that now form the New Testament.

16:16 Jesus was referring to his death, now only a few hours away, and his resurrection three days later.

¹⁹Jesus realized they wanted to ask him, so he said, "Are you asking yourselves what I meant? I said in just a little while I will be gone, and you won't see me anymore. Then, just a little while after that, you will see me again. ²⁰Truly, you will weep and mourn over what is going to happen to me, but the world will rejoice. You will grieve, but your grief will suddenly turn to wonderful joy when you see me again. ²¹It will be like a woman experiencing the pains of labor. When her child is born, her anguish gives place to joy because she has brought a new person into the world. ²²You have sorrow now, but I will see you again; then you will rejoice, and no one can rob you of that joy. ²³At that time you won't need to ask me for anything. The truth is, you can go directly to the Father and ask him, and he will grant your request because you use my name. ²⁴You haven't done this before. Ask, using my name, and you will receive, and you will have abundant joy.

²⁵"I have spoken of these matters in parables, but the time will come when this will not be necessary, and I will tell you plainly all about the Father. ²⁶Then you will ask in my name. I'm not saying I will ask the Father on your behalf, ²⁷for the Father himself loves you dearly because you love me and believe that I came from God. ²⁸Yes, I came from the Father into the world, and I will leave the world and return to the Father."

²⁹Then his disciples said, "At last you are speaking plainly and not in parables. ³⁰Now we understand that you know everything and don't need anyone to tell you anything.* From this we believe that you came from God."

³¹Jesus asked, "Do you finally believe? ³²But the time is coming—in fact, it is already here—when you will be scattered, each one going his own way, leaving me alone. Yet I am not alone because the Father is with me. ³³I have told you all this so that you may have peace in me. Here on earth you will have many trials and sorrows. But take heart, because I have overcome the world."

Jesus Prays for Himself (219)

17 When Jesus had finished saying all these things, he looked up to heaven and said, "Father, the time has come. Glorify your Son so he can give glory back to you. ²For you have given him authority over everyone in all the earth. He gives eternal life to each one you have given him. ³And this is the way to have eternal life—to know you, the only true God, and Jesus Christ, the one you sent to earth. ⁴I brought glory to you here on earth by doing everything you told me to do. ⁵And now, Father, bring me into the glory we shared before the world began.

16:30 Or *don't need that anyone should ask you anything.*

Cross references

16:20 Mark 16:10; Luke 23:27; John 20:20

16:21 Isa 13:8; 21:3; 26:17; Acts 13:33; Col 1:18

16:22 Isa 66:14; John 20:20

16:23 John 14:20; 16:26

16:24 John 15:11

16:25 Ps 78:2; John 10:6

16:27 John 8:42; 14:21; 17:8

16:28 John 13:3

16:32 Zech 13:7; Matt 26:31; John 8:29

16:33 John 14:27; Rom 5:1; 8:37; 1 Jn 5:4

17:1 John 13:31

17:2 Matt 28:18; John 6:37, 39

17:3 Phil 3:8; 1 Jn 5:20

17:5 John 1:1-2; 17:24; Phil 2:6

16:20 What a contrast between the disciples and the world! The world rejoiced as the disciples wept, but the disciples would see Jesus again (in three days) and rejoice. The world's values are often the opposite of God's values. This can cause Christians to feel like misfits. But even if life is difficult now, one day we will rejoice. Keep your eye on the future and on God's promises!

16:23-27 Jesus is talking about a new relationship between the believer and God. Previously, people approached God through priests. After Jesus' resurrection, any believer could approach God directly. A new day has dawned and now all believers are priests, talking with God personally and directly (see Hebrews 10:19-23). We approach God, not because of our own merit, but because Jesus, our great High Priest, has made us acceptable to God.

16:30 The disciples believed Jesus' words because they were convinced that he knew everything. But their belief was only a first step toward the great faith they would receive when the Holy Spirit came to live in them.

16:31-33 As Christians, we should expect continuing tension with an unbelieving world that is "out of sync" with Christ, his Good News, and his people. At the same time, we can expect our relationship with Christ to produce peace and comfort because we are "in sync" with him.

16:32 The disciples scattered after Jesus was arrested (see Mark 14:50).

16:33 Jesus summed up all he had told them this night, tying together themes from 14:27-29; 16:1-4; and 16:9-11. With these words he told his disciples to take courage. In spite of the inevitable struggles they would face, they would not be alone. Jesus does not abandon us to our struggles either. If we remember that the ultimate victory has already been won, we can claim the peace of Christ in the most troublesome times.

17:1ff This entire chapter is Jesus' prayer. From it, we learn that the world is a tremendous battleground where the forces under Satan's power and those under God's authority are at war. Satan and his forces are motivated by bitter hatred for Christ and his forces. Jesus prayed for his disciples, including those of us who follow him today. He prayed that God would keep his chosen believers safe from Satan's power, setting them apart and making them pure and holy, uniting them through his truth.

17:3 How do we get eternal life? Jesus tells us clearly here—by knowing God the Father himself through his Son, Jesus Christ. Eternal life requires entering into a personal relationship with God in Jesus Christ. When we admit our sin and turn away from it, Christ's love lives in us by the Holy Spirit.

17:5 Before Jesus came to earth, he was one with God. At this point, when his mission on earth was almost finished, Jesus was asking his Father to restore him to his original place of honor and authority. Jesus' resurrection and ascension—and Stephen's dying exclamation (Acts 7:56)—attest that Jesus did return to his exalted position at the right hand of God.

17:6
John 17:26

17:8
John 13:3; 16:30

17:9
1 Jn 5:19

17:10
John 16:15

17:11
John 10:30; 17:21
Gal 3:28

17:12
John 6:39

17:13
John 7:33; 15:11

17:14
John 15:18-19

17:15
1 Jn 5:18

17:17
John 15:3

17:18
John 20:21

17:19
Heb 2:11

17:20
John 17:9

17:21
John 10:38
Gal 3:28

17:22
John 17:11

17:23
John 16:27; 17:5

17:24
John 1:14; 12:26

Jesus Prays for His Disciples (220)

6"I have told these men about you. They were in the world, but then you gave them to me. Actually, they were always yours, and you gave them to me; and they have kept your word. 7Now they know that everything I have is a gift from you, 8for I have passed on to them the words you gave me; and they accepted them and know that I came from you, and they believe you sent me.

9"My prayer is not for the world, but for those you have given me, because they belong to you. 10And all of them, since they are mine, belong to you; and you have given them back to me, so they are my glory! 11Now I am departing the world; I am leaving them behind and coming to you. Holy Father, keep them and care for them—all those you have given me—so that they will be united just as we are. 12During my time here, I have kept them safe.* I guarded them so that not one was lost, except the one headed for destruction, as the Scriptures foretold.

13"And now I am coming to you. I have told them many things while I was with them so they would be filled with my joy. 14I have given them your word. And the world hates them because they do not belong to the world, just as I do not. 15I'm not asking you to take them out of the world, but to keep them safe from the evil one. 16They are not part of this world any more than I am. 17Make them pure and holy by teaching them your words of truth. 18As you sent me into the world, I am sending them into the world. 19And I give myself entirely to you so they also might be entirely yours.

Jesus Prays for Future Believers (221)

20"I am praying not only for these disciples but also for all who will ever believe in me because of their testimony. 21My prayer for all of them is that they will be one, just as you and I are one, Father—that just as you are in me and I am in you, so they will be in us, and the world will believe you sent me.

22"I have given them the glory you gave me, so that they may be one, as we are—23I in them and you in me, all being perfected into one. Then the world will know that you sent me and will understand that you love them as much as you love me. 24Father, I want these whom you've given me to be with me, so they can see my glory. You gave me the glory because you loved me even before the world began!

17:12 Greek *I have kept in your name those whom you have given me.*

17:10 What did Jesus mean when he said "they are my glory"? God's glory is the revelation of his character and presence. The lives of Jesus' disciples reveal his character, and he is present to the world through them. Does your life reveal Jesus' character and presence?

17:11 Jesus was asking that the disciples be united in harmony and love as the Father, Son, and Holy Spirit are united—the strongest of all unions. (See the notes on 17:21-23.)

17:12 Judas was the "one headed for destruction," who was lost because he betrayed Jesus and never sought forgiveness (see Psalm 41:9).

17:13 Joy is a common theme in Christ's teachings—he wants us to be joyful (see 15:11; 16:24). The key to immeasurable joy is living in intimate contact with Christ, the source of all joy. When we do, we will experience God's special care and protection and see the victory God brings even when defeat seems certain.

17:14 The world hates Christians because Christians' values differ from the world's. Because Christ's followers don't cooperate with the world by joining in their sin, they are living accusations against the world's immorality. The world follows Satan's agenda, and Satan is the avowed enemy of Jesus and his people.

17:17 A follower of Christ becomes pure and holy through believing and obeying the Word of God (Hebrews 4:12). He or she has already accepted forgiveness through Christ's sacrificial death (Hebrews 7:26, 27). But daily application of God's Word has a purifying effect on our minds and hearts. Scripture points out sin, motivates us to confess, renews our relationship with Christ, and guides us back to the right path.

17:18 Jesus didn't ask God to take believers *out* of the world but instead to use them *in* the world. Because Jesus sends us into the world, we should not try to escape from the world, nor should we avoid all relationships with non-Christians. We are called to be salt and light (Matthew 5:13-16), and we are to do the work that God sent us to do.

17:20 Jesus prayed for all who would follow him, including you and others you know. He prayed for unity (17:11), protection from the evil one (17:15), and holiness (17:17). Knowing that Jesus prayed for us should give us confidence as we work for his Kingdom.

17:21-23 Jesus' great desire for his disciples was that they would become one. He wanted them unified as a powerful witness to the reality of God's love. Are you helping to unify the body of Christ, the church? You can pray for other Christians, avoid gossip, build others up, work together in humility, give your time and money, exalt Christ, and refuse to get sidetracked arguing over divisive matters.

17:21-23 Jesus prayed for unity among believers based on the believers' unity with him and the Father. Christians can know unity among themselves if they are living in union with God. For example, each branch living in union with the vine is united with all other branches doing the same.

²⁵"O righteous Father, the world doesn't know you, but I do; and these disciples know you sent me. ²⁶And I have revealed you to them and will keep on revealing you. I will do this so that your love for me may be in them and I in them."

17:25
Matt 11:27

17:26
John 15:9

2. Jesus completes his mission

Jesus Is Betrayed and Arrested

(**224**/Matthew 26:47-56; Mark 14:43-52; Luke 22:47-53)

18 After saying these things, Jesus crossed the Kidron Valley with his disciples and entered a grove of olive trees. ²Judas, the betrayer, knew this place, because Jesus had gone there many times with his disciples. ³The leading priests and Pharisees had given Judas a battalion of Roman soldiers and Temple guards to accompany him. Now with blazing torches, lanterns, and weapons, they arrived at the olive grove.

18:1
2 Sam 15:23
Matt 26:36
Mark 14:32

18:3-11
//Matt 26:47-56
//Mark 14:43-50
//Luke 22:47-53

⁴Jesus fully realized all that was going to happen to him. Stepping forward to meet them, he asked, "Whom are you looking for?"

⁵"Jesus of Nazareth," they replied.

18:3
John 7:32, 45

18:4
John 6:64

"I am he,"* Jesus said. Judas was standing there with them when Jesus identified himself. ⁶And as he said, "I am he," they all fell backward to the ground! ⁷Once more he asked them, "Whom are you searching for?"

And again they replied, "Jesus of Nazareth."

⁸"I told you that I am he," Jesus said. "And since I am the one you want, let these others go." ⁹He did this to fulfill his own statement: "I have not lost a single one of those you gave me."*

18:9
John 6:39; 17:12

18:10
Luke 22:36, 38

¹⁰Then Simon Peter drew a sword and slashed off the right ear of Malchus, the high priest's servant. ¹¹But Jesus said to Peter, "Put your sword back into its sheath. Shall I not drink from the cup the Father has given me?"

18:11
Matt 20:22; 26:39
Mark 10:38; 14:36
Luke 22:42

18:5 Greek *I am;* also in 18:6, 8.   **18:9** See John 6:39 and 17:12.

18:3 The Jewish religious leaders were given authority by the Romans to make arrests for minor infractions. The Roman soldiers may not have participated in the arrest but accompanied the Temple guards to make sure matters didn't get out of control.

18:4, 5 John does not record Judas's kiss of greeting (Matthew 26:49; Mark 14:45; Luke 22:47, 48), but Judas's kiss marked a turning point for the disciples. With Jesus' arrest, each one's life would be radically different. For the first time, Judas openly betrayed Jesus before the other disciples. For the first time, Jesus' loyal disciples ran away from him (Matthew 26:56). The band of disciples would undergo severe testing before they were transformed from hesitant followers to dynamic leaders.

18:5, 6 The men may have been startled by the boldness of Jesus' question or by the words "I am he," a declaration of his divinity (Exodus 3:14). Or perhaps they were overcome by his obvious power and authority.

18:10, 11 Trying to protect Jesus, Peter pulled a sword and wounded the high priest's servant. But Jesus told Peter to put away his sword and allow God's plan to unfold. At times it is tempting to take matters into our own hands, to force the issue. Most often such moves lead to sin. Instead, we must trust God to work out his plan. Think of it—if Peter had had his way, Jesus would not have gone to the cross, and God's plan of redemption would have been thwarted.

18:11 "The cup" refers to the suffering, isolation, and death that Jesus would have to endure in order to atone for the sins of the world.

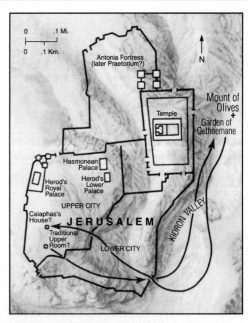

BETRAYAL IN THE GARDEN After eating the Passover meal in the upper room, Jesus and his disciples went to Gethsemane, where Judas led the Temple guard to arrest Jesus. Jesus was then taken to Caiaphas's house for his first of many trials.

Annas Questions Jesus (**225**)

18:12-14
//Matt 26:57-58
//Mark 14:53-54
//Luke 22:54

18:13
Luke 3:2
John 18:24

¹²So the soldiers, their commanding officer, and the Temple guards arrested Jesus and tied him up. ¹³First they took him to Annas, the father-in-law of Caiaphas, the high priest that year. ¹⁴Caiaphas was the one who had told the other Jewish leaders, "Better that one should die for all."

THE SIX STAGES OF JESUS' TRIAL Although Jesus' trial lasted less than 18 hours, he was taken to six different hearings.	BEFORE JEWISH AUTHORITIES	Preliminary Hearing before Annas (John 18:12–24)	Because the office of high priest was for life, Annas was still the "official" high priest in the eyes of the Jews, even though the Romans had appointed another. Thus, Annas still carried much weight in the high council.
		Hearing before Caiaphas (Matthew 26:57–68)	Like the hearing before Annas, this hearing was conducted at night in secrecy. It was full of illegalities that made a mockery of justice (see the chart in Matthew 28).
		Trial before the High Council (Matthew 27:1, 2)	Just after daybreak, 70 members of the high council met to rubber-stamp their approval of the previous hearings to make them appear legal. The purpose of this trial was not to determine justice, but to justify their own preconceptions of Jesus' guilt.
	BEFORE ROMAN AUTHORITIES	First Hearing before Pilate (Luke 23:1–5)	The religious leaders had condemned Jesus to death on religious grounds, but only the Roman government could grant the death penalty. Thus, they took Jesus to Pilate, the Roman governor, and accused him of treason and rebellion, crimes for which the Roman government gave the death penalty. Pilate saw at once that Jesus was innocent, but he was afraid about the uproar being caused by the religious leaders.
		Hearing before Herod (Luke 23:6–12)	Because Jesus' home was in the region of Galilee, Pilate sent Jesus to Herod Antipas, the ruler of Galilee, who was in Jerusalem for the Passover celebration. Herod was eager to see Jesus do a miracle, but when Jesus remained silent, Herod wanted nothing to do with him and sent him back to Pilate.
		Last Hearing before Pilate (Luke 23:13–25)	Pilate didn't like the religious leaders. He wasn't interested in condemning Jesus because he knew Jesus was innocent. However, he knew that another uprising in his district might cost him his job. First he tried to compromise with the religious leaders by having Jesus beaten, an illegal action in itself. But finally he gave in and handed Jesus over to be executed. Pilate's self-interest was stronger than his sense of justice.

18:12, 13 Jesus was immediately taken to the high priest's residence, even though this was the middle of the night. The religious leaders were in a hurry—they wanted to complete the execution before the Sabbath and get on with the Passover celebration. This residence was a palace whose outer walls enclosed a courtyard, where servants and soldiers could warm themselves around a fire.

18:13 Both Annas and Caiaphas had been high priests. Annas was Israel's high priest from A.D. 6 to 15, when he was deposed by Roman rulers. Caiaphas, Annas's son-in-law, was appointed high priest from A.D. 18 to 36/37. According to Jewish law, the office of high priest was held for life. Many Jews, therefore, still considered Annas the high priest and still called him by that title. But although Annas retained much authority among the Jews, Caiaphas made the final decisions.

Both Caiaphas and Annas cared more about their political ambitions than about their responsibility to lead the people to God. Though religious leaders, they had become evil. As the nation's spiritual leaders, they should have been sensitive to God's revelation. They should have known that Jesus was the Messiah about whom the Scriptures spoke, and they should have pointed the people to him. But when deceitful men and women pursue evil, they want to eliminate all opposition. Instead of honestly evaluating Jesus' claims based on their knowledge of Scripture, these religious leaders sought to further their own selfish ambitions and were even willing to kill God's Son, if that's what it took, to do it.

15Simon Peter followed along behind, as did another of the disciples. That other disciple was acquainted with the high priest, so he was allowed to enter the courtyard with Jesus. 16Peter stood outside the gate. Then the other disciple spoke to the woman watching at the gate, and she let Peter in. 17The woman asked Peter, "Aren't you one of Jesus' disciples?"

18:16-18
//Matt 26:69-70
//Mark 14:66-68
//Luke 22:55-57

"No," he said, "I am not."

18The guards and the household servants were standing around a charcoal fire they had made because it was cold. And Peter stood there with them, warming himself.

18:18
Mark 14:54, 67

19Inside, the high priest began asking Jesus about his followers and what he had been teaching them. 20Jesus replied, "What I teach is widely known, because I have preached regularly in the synagogues and the Temple. I have been heard by people* everywhere, and I teach nothing in private that I have not said in public. 21Why are you asking me this question? Ask those who heard me. They know what I said."

18:19-24
//Matt 26:59-68
//Mark 14:55-65
//Luke 22:63-71

18:20
Matt 26:55
John 7:26

22One of the Temple guards standing there struck Jesus on the face. "Is that the way to answer the high priest?" he demanded.

18:22
John 19:3

23Jesus replied, "If I said anything wrong, you must give evidence for it. Should you hit a man for telling the truth?"

18:23
Matt 5:39
Acts 23:2-5

24Then Annas bound Jesus and sent him to Caiaphas, the high priest.

18:24
Matt 26:3

Peter Denies Knowing Jesus
(**227**/Matthew 26:69-75; Mark 14:66-72; Luke 22:54-65)

25Meanwhile, as Simon Peter was standing by the fire, they asked him again, "Aren't you one of his disciples?"

18:25-27
//Matt 26:71-75
//Mark 14:69-72
//Luke 22:58-62

"I am not," he said.

26But one of the household servants of the high priest, a relative of the man whose ear

18:20 Greek *Jewish people;* also in 18:38.

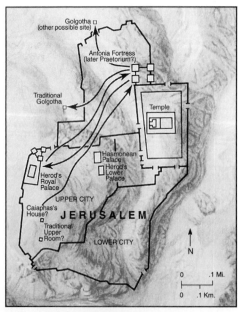

JESUS' TRIAL AND CRUCIFIXION Jesus was taken from trial before the Jewish high council to trial before the Roman governor, Pilate, in Pilate's palace. Pilate sent him to Herod (Luke 23:5–12), but Herod just returned Jesus to Pilate. Responding to threats from the mob, Pilate finally turned Jesus over to be crucified.

18:15, 16 The other disciple is probably John, the author of this Gospel. He knew the high priest and identified himself to the woman at the door. Because of his connections, John got himself and Peter into the courtyard. But Peter refused to identify himself as Jesus' follower. Peter's experiences in the next few hours would change his life. For more information about Peter, see his Profile in Matthew 27.

18:19ff During the night, Jesus had a pretrial hearing before Annas before he was taken to Caiaphas and the entire high council (Mark 14:53-65). The religious leaders knew they had no grounds for charging Jesus, so they tried to build evidence against him by using false witnesses (Mark 14:55-59).

18:22-27 We can easily get angry at the high council for their injustice in condemning Jesus, but we must remember that Peter and the rest of the disciples also contributed to Jesus' pain by deserting and denying him (Matthew 26:56, 75). While most of us are not like the religious leaders, we are all like the disciples, for all of us have been guilty of denying that Christ is Lord in vital areas of our lives or of keeping secret our identity as believers in times of pressure. Don't excuse yourself by pointing at others whose sins seem worse than yours. Instead, come to Jesus for forgiveness and healing.

18:25 The other three Gospels say that Peter's three denials happened near a fire in the courtyard outside Caiaphas's palace. John places the first denial outside Annas's home and the other two denials outside Caiaphas's home. This was very likely the same courtyard. The high priest's residence was large, and Annas and Caiaphas undoubtedly lived near each other.

18:25-27 Imagine standing outside while Jesus, your Lord and Master, is questioned. Imagine watching this man, whom you have come to believe is the long-awaited Messiah, being abused and beaten. Naturally Peter was confused and afraid. It is a serious sin to deny Christ, but Jesus forgave Peter (21:15-17). No sin is too great for Jesus to forgive if you are

18:27
John 13:38

Peter had cut off, asked, "Didn't I see you out there in the olive grove with Jesus?" ²⁷Again Peter denied it. And immediately a rooster crowed.

Jesus' Trial before Pilate (**230**/Matthew 27:11-14; Mark 15:2-5; Luke 23:1-5)

18:28-38
//Matt 27:1-2, 11-14
//Mark 15:1-5
//Luke 23:1-5

²⁸Jesus' trial before Caiaphas ended in the early hours of the morning. Then he was taken to the headquarters of the Roman governor. His accusers didn't go in themselves because it would defile them, and they wouldn't be allowed to celebrate the Passover feast. ²⁹So Pilate, the governor, went out to them and asked, "What is your charge against this man?"

³⁰"We wouldn't have handed him over to you if he weren't a criminal!" they retorted.

³¹"Then take him away and judge him by your own laws," Pilate told them.

"Only the Romans are permitted to execute someone," the Jewish leaders replied.

18:32
Matt 20:19
John 12:32

³²This fulfilled Jesus' prediction about the way he would die.*

18:33
Luke 23:3
John 19:9

³³Then Pilate went back inside and called for Jesus to be brought to him. "Are you the King of the Jews?" he asked him.

³⁴Jesus replied, "Is this your own question, or did others tell you about me?"

³⁵"Am I a Jew?" Pilate asked. "Your own people and their leading priests brought you here. Why? What have you done?"

18:36
Matt 26:53
Luke 17:21
John 6:15

³⁶Then Jesus answered, "I am not an earthly king. If I were, my followers would have fought when I was arrested by the Jewish leaders. But my Kingdom is not of this world."

³⁷Pilate replied, "You are a king then?"

18:37
John 8:47
1 Jn 4:6

"You say that I am a king, and you are right," Jesus said. "I was born for that purpose. And I came to bring truth to the world. All who love the truth recognize that what I say is true."

Pilate Hands Jesus Over to Be Crucified
(**232**/Matthew 27:15-26; Mark 15:6-15; Luke 23:13-25)

18:39–19:5
//Matt 27:15-31
//Mark 15:6-20
//Luke 23:13-25

³⁸"What is truth?" Pilate asked. Then he went out again to the people and told them, "He is not guilty of any crime. ³⁹But you have a custom of asking me to release

18:32 See John 12:32-33.

---

truly repentant. He will forgive even your worst sin if you turn from it and ask his pardon.

18:27 This fulfilled Jesus' words to Peter after he promised he would never deny him (Mark 14:31; John 13:38).

18:28 By Jewish law, entering the house of a Gentile would cause a Jewish person to be ceremonially defiled. As a result, he could not take part in worship at the Temple or celebrate the festivals until he was restored to a state of "cleanness." Afraid of being defiled, these men stayed outside the house where they had taken Jesus for trial. They kept the ceremonial requirements of their religion while harboring murder and treachery in their hearts.

18:29 This Roman governor, Pilate, was in charge of Judea (the region where Jerusalem was located) from A.D. 26 to 36. Pilate was unpopular with the Jews because he had raided the Temple treasuries for money to build an aqueduct. He did not like the Jews, but when Jesus, the King of the Jews, stood before him, Pilate found him innocent.

18:30 Pilate knew what was going on; he knew that the religious leaders hated Jesus, and he did not want to act as their executioner. They could not sentence him to death themselves—permission had to come from a Roman leader. But Pilate initially refused to sentence Jesus without sufficient evidence. Jesus' life became a pawn in a political power struggle.

18:31ff Pilate made four attempts to deal with Jesus: (1) He tried to put the responsibility on someone else (18:31); (2) he tried to find a way of escape so he could release Jesus (18:39); (3) he tried to compromise by having Jesus flogged rather than handing him over to die (19:1-3); and (4) he tried a direct appeal to the sympathy of the accusers (19:15). Everyone has to decide

what to do with Jesus. Pilate tried to let everyone else decide for him—and in the end, he lost.

18:32 This prediction is recorded in Matthew 20:19 and John 12:32, 35. Crucifixion was a common method of execution for criminals who were not Roman citizens.

18:34 If Pilate was asking this question in his role as the Roman governor, he would have been inquiring whether Jesus was setting up a rebel government. But the Jews were using the word *king* to mean their religious ruler, the Messiah. Israel was a captive nation, under the authority of the Roman Empire. A rival king might have threatened Rome; a Messiah could have been a purely religious leader.

18:36, 37 Pilate asked Jesus a straightforward question, and Jesus answered clearly. Jesus is a King, but one whose Kingdom is not of this world. There seems to have been no question in Pilate's mind that Jesus spoke the truth and was innocent of any crime. It also seems apparent that while recognizing the truth, Pilate chose to reject it. It is a tragedy when we fail to recognize the truth. It is a greater tragedy when we recognize the truth but fail to heed it.

18:38 Pilate was cynical; he thought that all truth was relative. To many government officials, truth was whatever the majority of people agreed with or whatever helped advance their own personal power and political goals. When there is no basis for truth, there is no basis for moral right and wrong. Justice becomes whatever works or whatever helps those in power. In Jesus and his Word we have a standard for truth and for our moral behavior.

someone from prison each year at Passover. So if you want me to, I'll release the King of the Jews."

⁴⁰But they shouted back, "No! Not this man, but Barabbas!" (Barabbas was a criminal.)

19 Then Pilate had Jesus flogged with a lead-tipped whip. ²The soldiers made a crown of long, sharp thorns and put it on his head, and they put a royal purple robe on him. ³"Hail! King of the Jews!" they mocked, and they hit him with their fists.

⁴Pilate went outside again and said to the people, "I am going to bring him out to you now, but understand clearly that I find him not guilty." ⁵Then Jesus came out wearing the crown of thorns and the purple robe. And Pilate said, "Here is the man!"

⁶When they saw him, the leading priests and Temple guards began shouting, "Crucify! Crucify!"

"You crucify him," Pilate said. "I find him not guilty."

⁷The Jewish leaders replied, "By our laws he ought to die because he called himself the Son of God."

⁸When Pilate heard this, he was more frightened than ever. ⁹He took Jesus back into the headquarters again and asked him, "Where are you from?" But Jesus gave no answer. ¹⁰"You won't talk to me?" Pilate demanded. "Don't you realize that I have the power to release you or to crucify you?"

¹¹Then Jesus said, "You would have no power over me at all unless it were given to you from above. So the one who brought me to you has the greater sin."

¹²Then Pilate tried to release him, but the Jewish leaders told him, "If you release this man, you are not a friend of Caesar. Anyone who declares himself a king is a rebel against Caesar."

¹³When they said this, Pilate brought Jesus out to them again. Then Pilate sat down on the judgment seat on the platform that is called the Stone Pavement (in Hebrew, *Gabbatha*). ¹⁴It was now about noon of the day of preparation for the Passover. And Pilate said to the people,* "Here is your king!"

19:14 Greek *Jewish people;* also in 19:20.

Marginal cross-references:
19:1 Isa 50:6; 53:5
19:3 John 18:22
19:4 Luke 23:4; John 18:38
19:6 John 18:31
19:7 Lev 24:16; Matt 26:63-66
19:11 Rom 13:1
19:12 Luke 23:2; Acts 17:7
19:13 Matt 27:19

18:40 Barabbas was a rebel against Rome, and although he had committed murder, he was probably a hero among the Jews. The Jews hated being governed by Rome and paying taxes to the despised government. Barabbas, who had led a rebellion and failed, was released instead of Jesus, the only one who could truly help Israel. For more on Barabbas, see the note on Luke 23:18, 19.

19:1ff To grasp the full picture of Jesus' crucifixion, read John's perspective along with the other three accounts in Matthew 27, Mark 15, and Luke 23. Each writer adds meaningful details, but each has the same message—Jesus died on the cross, in fulfillment of Old Testament prophecy, so that we could be saved from our sins and be given eternal life.

19:1-3 Flogging could have killed Jesus. The usual procedure was to bare the upper half of the victim's body and tie his hands to a pillar before whipping him with a three-pronged whip, with pieces of lead in the prongs. The number of lashes was determined by the severity of the crime; up to 40 were permitted under Jewish law (Deuteronomy 25:3). After being flogged, Jesus also endured other agonies recorded here and in the other Gospels.

19:2-5 The soldiers went beyond their orders to whip Jesus—they also mocked his claim to royalty by placing a crown on his head and a royal robe on his shoulders.

19:7 The truth finally came out—the religious leaders had not brought Jesus to Pilate because he was causing rebellion against Rome, but because they thought he had broken their religious laws. Blasphemy, one of the most serious crimes in Jewish law, deserved the death penalty. Accusing Jesus of blasphemy would give credibility to their case in the eyes of Jews; accusing Jesus of treason would give credibility to their case in the eyes of the Romans. They didn't care which accusation Pilate listened to, as long as he would cooperate with them in killing Jesus.

19:10 Throughout the trial we see that Jesus was in control, not Pilate or the religious leaders. Pilate vacillated, the Jewish leaders reacted out of hatred and anger, but Jesus remained composed. He knew the truth, he knew God's plan, and he knew the reason for his trial. Despite the pressure and persecution, Jesus remained unmoved. It was really Pilate and the religious leaders who were on trial, not Jesus. When you are questioned or ridiculed because of your faith, remember that while you may be on trial before your accusers, they are on trial before God.

19:11 When Jesus said the man who delivered him to Pilate was guiltier than Pilate, he was not excusing Pilate for reacting to the political pressure placed on him. Pilate was responsible for his decision about Jesus. Caiaphas and the other religious leaders were guilty of a greater sin because they premeditated Jesus' murder.

19:12, 13 These words pressured Pilate into allowing Jesus to be crucified. As Roman governor of the area, Pilate was expected to keep the peace. Because Rome could not afford to keep large numbers of troops in the outlying regions, they maintained control by crushing rebellions immediately with brute force. Pilate was afraid that reports to Caesar of insurrection in his region would cost Pilate his job and perhaps even his life. When we face a tough decision, we can take the easy way out, or we can stand for what is right regardless of the cost. If we know the good we ought to do and don't do it, we sin (James 4:17).

19:13 The Stone Pavement was part of the Tower of Antonia bordering the northwest corner of the Temple complex.

19:16-27
//Matt 27:32-44
//Mark 15:21-32
//Luke 23:26-43

[15]"Away with him," they yelled. "Away with him—crucify him!"

"What? Crucify your king?" Pilate asked.

"We have no king but Caesar," the leading priests shouted back. [16]Then Pilate gave Jesus to them to be crucified.

Jesus Is Led Away to Be Crucified
(234/Matthew 27:32-37; Mark 15:21-24; Luke 23:26-31)

So they took Jesus and led him away. [17]Carrying the cross by himself, Jesus went to the place called Skull Hill (in Hebrew, *Golgotha*).

Jesus Is Placed on the Cross **(235**/Matthew 27:35-44; Mark 15:25-32; Luke 23:32-43)
[18]There they crucified him. There were two others crucified with him, one on either side, with Jesus between them. [19]And Pilate posted a sign over him that read, "Jesus of Nazareth, the King of the Jews." [20]The place where Jesus was crucified was near the city; and the sign was written in Hebrew, Latin, and Greek, so that many people could read it.

[21]Then the leading priests said to Pilate, "Change it from 'The King of the Jews' to 'He said, I am King of the Jews.'"

[22]Pilate replied, "What I have written, I have written. It stays exactly as it is."

19:24
†Ps 22:18

19:25
Matt 27:55-56
Mark 15:40-41
Luke 8:2; 23:49

[23]When the soldiers had crucified Jesus, they divided his clothes among the four of them. They also took his robe, but it was seamless, woven in one piece from the top. [24]So they said, "Let's not tear it but throw dice* to see who gets it." This fulfilled the Scripture that says, "They divided my clothes among themselves and threw dice for my robe."* [25]So that is what they did.

19:26
John 2:4; 13:23;
20:2; 21:7, 20

Standing near the cross were Jesus' mother, and his mother's sister, Mary (the wife of Clopas), and Mary Magdalene. [26]When Jesus saw his mother standing there beside the disciple he loved, he said to her, "Woman, he is your son." [27]And he said to this disciple, "She is your mother." And from then on this disciple took her into his home.

19:28-37
//Matt 27:45-56
//Mark 15:33-41
//Luke 23:44-49

Jesus Dies on the Cross **(236**/Matthew 27:45-56; Mark 15:33-41; Luke 23:44-49)
[28]Jesus knew that everything was now finished, and to fulfill the Scriptures he said, "I am thirsty."* [29]A jar of sour wine was sitting there, so they soaked a sponge in it, put it

19:28
†Pss 22:15; 69:21

19:24a Greek *cast lots.*   **19:24b** Ps 22:18.   **19:28** See Pss 22:15; 69:21.

19:15 The Jewish leaders were so desperate to get rid of Jesus that, despite their intense hatred for Rome, they shouted, "We have no king but Caesar." How ironic that they feigned allegiance to Rome while rejecting their own Messiah! Their own words condemned them, for God was to be their only true King, and they had abandoned every trace of loyalty to him. The priests had truly lost their reason for existence—instead of turning people to God, they claimed allegiance to Rome in order to kill their Messiah.

19:17 This place called Skull Hill was probably a hill outside Jerusalem along a main road. Many executions took place here so the Romans could use them as an example to the people.

19:18 Crucifixion was a Roman form of execution. The condemned man was forced to carry his cross along a main road to the execution site, as a warning to the people. Types of crosses and methods of crucifixion varied. Jesus was nailed to his cross; some people were tied with ropes. Death came by suffocation because the weight of the body made breathing difficult as the victim lost strength. Crucifixion was a hideously slow and painful death.

19:19 This sign was meant to be ironic. A king, stripped nearly naked and executed in public view, had obviously lost his kingdom forever. But Jesus, who turns the world's wisdom upside down, was just coming into his Kingdom. His death and resurrection would strike the deathblow to Satan's rule and would establish Jesus' eternal authority over the earth. Few people reading the sign that bleak afternoon understood its real meaning, but the sign was absolutely true. All was not lost. Jesus was King of the Jews—and of the Gentiles, and of the whole universe.

19:20 The sign was written in three languages: Hebrew for the native Jews, Latin for the Roman occupation forces, and Greek for foreigners and Jews visiting from other lands.

19:23, 24 Roman soldiers in charge of crucifixions customarily took for themselves the clothes of the condemned men. They divided Jesus' clothing, throwing dice to determine who would get his seamless garment, the most valuable piece of clothing. This fulfilled the prophecy in Psalm 22:18.

19:25-27 Even while dying on the cross, Jesus was concerned about his family. He instructed John to care for Mary, Jesus' mother. Our families are precious gifts from God, and we should value and care for them under all circumstances. Neither Christian work nor key responsibilities in any job or position excuse us from caring for our families. What can you do today to show your love to your family?

19:27 Jesus asked his close friend John, the writer of this Gospel, to care for Jesus' mother, Mary, whose husband, Joseph, must have been dead by this time. Why didn't Jesus assign this task to his brothers? As the oldest son, Jesus entrusted his mother to a person who stayed with him at the cross—and that was John.

19:29 This sour wine was a cheap wine that the Roman soldiers drank while waiting for those crucified to die.

on a hyssop branch, and held it up to his lips. ³⁰When Jesus had tasted it, he said, "It is finished!" Then he bowed his head and gave up his spirit.

³¹The Jewish leaders didn't want the victims hanging there the next day, which was the Sabbath (and a very special Sabbath at that, because it was the Passover), so they asked Pilate to hasten their deaths by ordering that their legs be broken. Then their bodies could be taken down. ³²So the soldiers came and broke the legs of the two men crucified with Jesus. ³³But when they came to Jesus, they saw that he was dead already, so they didn't break his legs. ³⁴One of the soldiers, however, pierced his side with a spear, and blood and water flowed out. ³⁵This report is from an eyewitness giving an accurate account; it is presented so that you also can believe. ³⁶These things happened in fulfillment of the Scriptures that say, "Not one of his bones will be broken,"* ³⁷and "They will look on him whom they pierced."*

Jesus Is Laid in the Tomb (**237**/Matthew 27:57-61; Mark 15:42-47; Luke 23:50-56)

³⁸Afterward Joseph of Arimathea, who had been a secret disciple of Jesus (because he feared the Jewish leaders), asked Pilate for permission to take Jesus' body down. When Pilate gave him permission, he came and took the body away. ³⁹Nicodemus, the man who had come to Jesus at night, also came, bringing about seventy-five pounds* of embalming ointment made from myrrh and aloes. ⁴⁰Together they wrapped Jesus' body in a long linen cloth with the spices, as is the Jewish custom of burial. ⁴¹The place of crucifixion was near a garden, where there was a new tomb, never used before. ⁴²And so, because it was the day of preparation before the Passover and since the tomb was close at hand, they laid Jesus there.

19:36 Exod 12:46; Num 9:12; Ps 34:20.   **19:37** Zech 12:10.   **19:39** Greek *100 litras* [32.7 kilograms].

19:30
Job 19:26-27

19:31
Deut 21:22-23

19:35
John 20:30-31;
21:24
1 Jn 1:1

19:36
†Exod 12:46
Num 9:12
†Ps 34:20

19:37
†Zech 12:10
Rev 1:7

19:38-42
∥Matt 27:57-61
∥Mark 15:42-47
∥Luke 23:50-56

19:39
John 3:1-2; 7:50

19:40
Luke 24:12
John 20:5-7

19:30 Until this time, a complicated system of sacrifices had atoned for sins. Sin separates people from God, and only through the sacrifice of an animal, a substitute, could people be forgiven and become clean before God. But people sin continually, so frequent sacrifices were required. Jesus, however, became the final and ultimate sacrifice for sin. The word *finished* is the same as "paid in full." Jesus came to *finish* God's work of salvation (4:34; 17:4), to pay the full penalty for our sins. With his death, the complex sacrificial system ended because Jesus took all sin upon himself. Now we can freely approach God because of what Jesus did for us. Those who believe in Jesus' death and resurrection can live eternally with God and escape the penalty that comes from sin.

19:31 It was against God's law to leave the body of a dead person exposed overnight (Deuteronomy 21:23), and it was also against the law to work after sundown on Friday, when the Sabbath began. This is why the religious leaders urgently wanted to get Jesus' body off the cross and buried by sundown.

19:31-35 These Romans were experienced soldiers. They knew from many previous crucifixions whether a man was dead or alive. There was no question that Jesus was dead when they checked him, so they decided not to break his legs as they had done to the other victims. Piercing his side and seeing the sudden flow of blood and water (indicating that the sac surrounding the heart and the heart itself had been pierced) was further proof of his death. Some people say Jesus didn't really die, that he only passed out—and that's how he came back to life. But we have the witness of an impartial party, the Roman soldiers, that Jesus died on the cross (see Mark 15:44, 45).

19:32 The Roman soldiers would break victims' legs to hasten the death process. When a person hung on a cross, death came by suffocation, but the victim could push against the cross with his legs to hold up his body and keep breathing. With broken legs, he would suffocate almost immediately.

19:34, 35 The graphic details of Jesus' death are especially important in John's record because he was an eyewitness.

19:36, 37 Jesus died as the lambs for the Passover meal were being slain. Not a bone was to be broken in these sacrificial lambs (Exodus 12:46; Numbers 9:12). Jesus, the Lamb of God, was the perfect sacrifice for the sins of the world (1 Corinthians 5:7).

19:38, 39 Four people were changed in the process of Jesus' death. The criminal, dying on the cross beside Jesus, asked Jesus to include him in his Kingdom (Luke 23:39-43). The Roman officer proclaimed that Jesus was surely the Son of God (Mark 15:39). Joseph and Nicodemus, members of the Jewish high council and secret followers of Jesus (7:50-52), came out of hiding. These men were changed more by Jesus' death than by his life. They realized who Jesus was, and that realization brought out their belief, proclamation, and action. When confronted with Jesus and his death, we should be changed—to believe, proclaim, and act.

19:38-42 Joseph of Arimathea and Nicodemus were secret followers of Jesus. They were afraid to make this allegiance known because of their positions in the Jewish community. Joseph was a leader and honored member of the Jewish high council. Nicodemus, also a member of the high council, had come to Jesus by night (3:1) and later tried to defend him before the other religious leaders (7:50-52). Yet they risked their reputations to provide for Jesus' burial. Are you a secret believer? Do you hide your faith from your friends and fellow workers? This is an appropriate time to step out of hiding and let others know whom you follow.

19:42 This tomb was probably a cave carved out of the stone hillside. It was large enough for a person to walk into, so Joseph and Nicodemus carried Jesus' body into it. A large stone was rolled in front of the entrance.

19:42 As they buried Jesus, Nicodemus and Joseph had to hurry to avoid working on the Sabbath, which began Friday evening at sundown.

Jeus Rises from the Dead (**239**/Matthew 28:1-7; Mark 16:1-8; Luke 24:1-12)

20:1-8
//Matt 28:1-8
//Mark 16:1-8
//Luke 24:1-12

20:2
John 13:23

20:3
Luke 24:12

20:5
John 19:40

20:7
John 11:44

20 Early Sunday morning,* while it was still dark, Mary Magdalene came to the tomb and found that the stone had been rolled away from the entrance. ²She ran and found Simon Peter and the other disciple, the one whom Jesus loved. She said, "They have taken the Lord's body out of the tomb, and I don't know where they have put him!"

³Peter and the other disciple ran to the tomb to see. ⁴The other disciple outran Peter and got there first. ⁵He stooped and looked in and saw the linen cloth lying there, but he didn't go in. ⁶Then Simon Peter arrived and went inside. He also noticed the linen wrappings lying there, ⁷while the cloth that had covered Jesus' head was folded up and lying to the side. ⁸Then the other disciple also went in, and he saw and believed—

20:1 Greek *On the first day of the week.*

MARY MAGDALENE

The absence of women among the 12 disciples has bothered a few people. But it is clear that there were many women among Jesus' followers. It is also clear that Jesus did not treat women as others in his culture did; he treated them with dignity, as people with worth.

Mary of Magdala was an early follower of Jesus who certainly deserves to be called a disciple. An energetic, impulsive, caring woman, she not only traveled with Jesus, but also contributed to the needs of the group. She was present at the Crucifixion and was on her way to anoint Jesus' body on Sunday morning when she discovered the empty tomb. Mary was the first to see Jesus after his resurrection.

Mary Magdalene is a heartwarming example of thankful living. Her life was miraculously freed by Jesus when he drove seven demons out of her. In every glimpse we have of her, she was acting out her appreciation for the freedom Christ had given her. That freedom allowed her to stand under Christ's cross when all the disciples except John were hiding in fear. After Jesus' death, she intended to give his body every respect. Like the rest of Jesus' followers, she never expected his bodily resurrection— but she was overjoyed to discover it.

Mary's faith was not complicated, but it was direct and genuine. She was more eager to believe and obey than to understand everything. Jesus honored her childlike faith by appearing to her first and by entrusting her with the first message of his resurrection.

Strengths and accomplishments	• Contributed to the needs of Jesus and his disciples • One of the few faithful followers present at Jesus' death on the cross • First to see the risen Christ
Weakness and mistake	• Jesus had to drive seven demons out of her
Lessons from her life	• Those who are obedient grow in understanding • Women are vital to Jesus' ministry • Jesus relates to women as he created them—as equal reflectors of God's image
Vital statistics	• Where: Magdala, Jerusalem • Occupation: We are not told, but she seems to have been wealthy • Contemporaries: Jesus, the 12 disciples, Mary, Martha, Lazarus, Jesus' mother Mary
Key verse	"It was early on Sunday morning when Jesus rose from the dead, and the first person who saw him was Mary Magdalene, the woman from whom he had cast out seven demons" (Mark 16:9).

Mary Magdalene's story is told in Matthew 27—28; Mark 15—16; Luke 23—24; and John 19—20. She is also mentioned in Luke 8:2.

20:1 Other women came to the tomb along with Mary Magdalene. The other Gospel accounts give their names. For more information on Mary Magdalene, see her Profile in chapter 20.

20:1 The stone was not rolled away from the entrance to the tomb so Jesus could get out. He could have left easily without moving the stone. It was rolled away so others could get *in* and see that Jesus was gone.

20:1ff People who hear about the Resurrection for the first time may need time before they can comprehend this amazing story. Like Mary and the disciples, they may pass through four stages of belief. (1) At first, they may think the story is a fabrication, impossible to believe (20:2). (2) Like Peter, they may check out the facts and still be puzzled about what happened (20:6). (3) Only when they encounter Jesus personally are they able to accept the fact of the Resurrection (20:16). (4) Then, as they commit themselves to the risen Lord and devote their lives to serving him, they begin to understand fully the reality of his presence with them (20:28).

20:7 The linen wrappings were left as if Jesus had passed right through them. The cloth that covered Jesus' head was still rolled up in the shape of a head, and it was at about the right distance from the wrappings that had enveloped Jesus' body. A grave robber couldn't possibly have made off with Jesus' body and left the linens as if they were still shaped around it.

⁹for until then they hadn't realized that the Scriptures said he would rise from the dead. ¹⁰Then they went home.

*Jesus Appears to Mary Magdalene (**240**/Mark 16:9-11)*
¹¹Mary was standing outside the tomb crying, and as she wept, she stooped and looked in. ¹²She saw two white-robed angels sitting at the head and foot of the place where the body of Jesus had been lying. ¹³"Why are you crying?" the angels asked her.

"Because they have taken away my Lord," she replied, "and I don't know where they have put him."

¹⁴She glanced over her shoulder and saw someone standing behind her. It was Jesus, but she didn't recognize him. ¹⁵"Why are you crying?" Jesus asked her. "Who are you looking for?"

She thought he was the gardener. "Sir," she said, "if you have taken him away, tell me where you have put him, and I will go and get him."

¹⁶"Mary!" Jesus said.

She turned toward him and exclaimed, "Teacher!"*

¹⁷"Don't cling to me," Jesus said, "for I haven't yet ascended to the Father. But go find my brothers and tell them that I am ascending to my Father and your Father, my God and your God."

¹⁸Mary Magdalene found the disciples and told them, "I have seen the Lord!" Then she gave them his message.

*Jesus Appears to His Disciples (**244**/Luke 24:36-43)*
¹⁹That evening, on the first day of the week, the disciples were meeting behind locked doors because they were afraid of the Jewish leaders. Suddenly, Jesus was standing there among them! "Peace be with you," he said. ²⁰As he spoke, he held out his hands for them to see, and he showed them his side. They were filled with joy when they saw their Lord! ²¹He spoke to them again and said, "Peace be with you. As the Father has sent me, so I send you." ²²Then he breathed on them and said to them, "Receive the Holy Spirit. ²³If you forgive anyone's sins, they are forgiven. If you refuse to forgive them, they are unforgiven."

20:16 Greek *and said in Hebrew, "Rabboni," which means "Teacher."*

Side references: 20:9 John 2:22 · 20:11-18 Mark 16:9-11 · 20:12 Mark 16:5, Luke 24:4 · 20:14 Mark 16:9, Luke 24:16, John 21:4 · 20:17 Matt 28:10, John 16:28, Rom 8:29, Col 1:18, Heb 2:11 · 20:19-23 //Matt 28:16-20, //Luke 24:36-49 · 20:20 John 16:20-22 · 20:21 Matt 28:19, John 17:18 · 20:22 John 7:37-39; 14:16-18, 26

20:9 As further proof that the disciples did not fabricate this story, we find that Peter and John were surprised that Jesus was not in the tomb. When John saw the linen wrappings looking like an empty cocoon from which Jesus had emerged, he believed that Jesus had risen. It wasn't until after they had seen the empty tomb that they remembered what the Scriptures and Jesus had said—he would die, but he would also rise again!

20:9 Jesus' resurrection is the key to the Christian faith. Why? (1) Just as he said, Jesus rose from the dead. We can be confident, therefore, that he will accomplish all he has promised. (2) Jesus' bodily resurrection shows us that the living Christ, not a false prophet or imposter, is ruler of God's eternal Kingdom. (3) We can be certain of our own resurrection because Jesus was resurrected. Death is not the end—there is future life. (4) The divine power that brought Jesus back to life is now available to us to bring our spiritually dead selves back to life. (5) The Resurrection is the basis for the church's witness to the world.

20:17 Mary did not want to lose Jesus again. She had not yet understood the Resurrection. Perhaps she thought this was his promised second coming (14:3). But Jesus did not want to be detained at the tomb. If he did not ascend to heaven, the Holy Spirit could not come. Both he and Mary had important work to do.

20:18 Mary didn't recognize Jesus at first. Her grief had blinded her; she couldn't see him because she didn't expect to see him. Then he spoke her name, and immediately she recognized him. Imagine the love that flooded her heart when she heard her Savior saying her name. Jesus is near you, and he is calling your name. Can you, like Mary, regard him as your Lord?

20:18 Mary did not meet the risen Christ until she had discovered the empty tomb. She responded with joy and obedience by going to tell the disciples. We cannot meet Christ until we discover that he is indeed alive, that his tomb is empty. Are you filled with joy by this good news, and do you share it with others?

20:21 Jesus again identified himself with his Father. He told the disciples by whose authority he did his work. Then he passed the job to his disciples of spreading the Good News of salvation around the world. Whatever God has asked you to do, remember: (1) Your authority comes from God, and (2) Jesus has demonstrated by words and actions how to accomplish the job he has given you. As the Father sent Jesus, Jesus sends his followers . . . and you.

20:22 This may have been a special filling of the Holy Spirit for the disciples, a foretaste of what all believers would experience from the time of Pentecost (Acts 2) and forever after. To do God's work, we need the guidance and power of the Holy Spirit. We must avoid trying to do his work in our own strength.

20:22 There is life in the breath of God. Man was created but did not come alive until God breathed into him the breath of life (Genesis 2:7). God's first breath made man different from all other forms of creation. Now, through the breath of Jesus, God imparted eternal, spiritual life. With this inbreathing came the power to do God's will on earth.

Jesus Appears to Thomas (**245**/Mark 16:14)

20:24
John 11:16

²⁴One of the disciples, Thomas (nicknamed the Twin*), was not with the others when Jesus came. ²⁵They told him, "We have seen the Lord!" But he replied, "I won't believe it unless I see the nail wounds in his hands, put my fingers into them, and place my hand into the wound in his side."

20:24 Greek *the one who was called Didymus.*

THOMAS

Thomas, so often remembered as "Doubting Thomas," deserves to be respected for his faith. He was a doubter, but his doubts had a purpose—he wanted to know the truth. Thomas did not idolize his doubts; he gladly believed when given reasons to do so. He expressed his doubts fully and had them answered completely. Doubting was only his way of responding, not his way of life.

Although our glimpses of Thomas are brief, his character comes through with consistency. He struggled to be faithful to what he knew, despite what he felt. At one point, when it was plain to everyone that Jesus' life was in danger, only Thomas put into words what most were feeling, "Let's go, too—and die with Jesus" (John 11:16). He didn't hesitate to follow Jesus.

We don't know why Thomas was absent the first time Jesus appeared to the disciples after the Resurrection, but he was reluctant to believe their witness to Christ's resurrection. Not even 10 friends could change his mind!

We can doubt without having to live a doubting way of life. Doubt encourages rethinking. Its purpose is more to sharpen the mind than to change it. Doubt can be used to pose the question, get an answer, and push for a decision. But doubt was never meant to be a permanent condition. Doubt is one foot lifted, poised to step forward or backward. There is no motion until the foot comes down.

When you experience doubt, take encouragement from Thomas. He didn't stay in his doubt but allowed Jesus to bring him to belief. Take encouragement also from the fact that countless other followers of Christ have struggled with doubts. The answers God gave them may help you, too. Don't settle into doubts, but move on from them to decision and belief. Find another believer with whom you can share your doubts. Silent doubts rarely find answers.

Strengths and accomplishments	• One of Jesus' 12 disciples • Intense both in doubt and belief • Was a loyal and honest man
Weaknesses and mistakes	• Along with the others, abandoned Jesus at his arrest • Refused to believe the others' claims to have seen Christ and demanded proof • Struggled with a pessimistic outlook
Lessons from his life	• Jesus does not reject doubts that are honest and directed toward belief • Better to doubt out loud than to disbelieve in silence
Vital statistics	• Where: Galilee, Judea, Samaria • Occupation: Disciple of Jesus • Contemporaries: Jesus, other disciples, Herod, Pilate
Key verses	"Then he said to Thomas, 'Put your finger here and see my hands. Put your hand into the wound in my side. Don't be faithless any longer. Believe!' 'My Lord and my God!' Thomas exclaimed" (John 20:27, 28).

Thomas's story is told in the Gospels. He is also mentioned in Acts 1:13.

20:23 Jesus was giving the disciples their Spirit-powered and Spirit-guided mission—to preach the Good News about Jesus so people's sins might be forgiven. The disciples did not have the power to forgive sins (only God can forgive sins), but Jesus gave them the privilege of telling new believers that their sins *have been* forgiven because they have accepted Jesus' message (see the note on Matthew 16:19). All believers have this same privilege. We can announce forgiveness of sins with certainty when we ourselves have found repentance and faith.

20:24-29 Have you ever wished you could actually see Jesus, touch him, and hear his words? Are there times you want to sit down with him and get his advice? Thomas wanted Jesus' physical presence. But God's plan is wiser. He has not limited himself to one physical body; he wants to be present with you at all times. Even now he is with you in the form of the

Holy Spirit. You can talk to him, and you can find his words to you in the pages of the Bible. He can be as real to you as he was to Thomas.

20:25-28 Jesus wasn't hard on Thomas for his doubts. Despite his skepticism, Thomas was still loyal to the believers and to Jesus himself. Some people need to doubt before they believe. If doubt leads to questions, questions lead to answers, and the answers are accepted, then doubt has done good work. It is when doubt becomes stubbornness and stubbornness becomes a life-style that doubt harms faith. When you doubt, don't stop there. Let your doubt deepen your faith as you continue to search for the answer.

26 Eight days later the disciples were together again, and this time Thomas was with them. The doors were locked; but suddenly, as before, Jesus was standing among them. He said, "Peace be with you." 27 Then he said to Thomas, "Put your finger here and see my hands. Put your hand into the wound in my side. Don't be faithless any longer. Believe!"

20:28
John 1:1, 18;
10:30; 14:9
Phil 2:6
Col 2:9
Titus 2:13
2 Pet 1:1
1 Jn 5:20

28 "My Lord and my God!" Thomas exclaimed.

29 Then Jesus told him, "You believe because you have seen me. Blessed are those who haven't seen me and believe anyway."

20:29
1 Pet 1:8

30 Jesus' disciples saw him do many other miraculous signs besides the ones recorded in this book. 31 But these are written so that you may believe* that Jesus is the Messiah, the Son of God, and that by believing in him you will have life.

20:30
John 21:25

20:31
John 3:15; 19:35
1 Jn 5:13

Jesus Appears to Seven Disciples (**246**)

21 Later Jesus appeared again to the disciples beside the Sea of Galilee.* This is how it happened. 2 Several of the disciples were there—Simon Peter, Thomas (nicknamed the Twin*), Nathanael from Cana in Galilee, the sons of Zebedee, and two other disciples.

21:2
John 1:45-51;
11:16; 20:24

3 Simon Peter said, "I'm going fishing."

"We'll come, too," they all said. So they went out in the boat, but they caught nothing all night.

21:3
Luke 5:5

4 At dawn the disciples saw Jesus standing on the beach, but they couldn't see who he was. 5 He called out, "Friends, have you caught any fish?"

21:4
Luke 24:16
John 20:14

"No," they replied.

6 Then he said, "Throw out your net on the right-hand side of the boat, and you'll get plenty of fish!" So they did, and they couldn't draw in the net because there were so many fish in it.

21:6
Luke 5:4-7

7 Then the disciple whom Jesus loved said to Peter, "It is the Lord!" When Simon Peter heard that it was the Lord, he put on his tunic (for he had stripped for work), jumped into the water, and swam ashore. 8 The others stayed with the boat and pulled the loaded net to the shore, for they were only out about three hundred feet.* 9 When they got there, they saw that a charcoal fire was burning and fish were frying over it, and there was bread.

21:7
John 13:23

21:9
John 18:18

10 "Bring some of the fish you've just caught," Jesus said. 11 So Simon Peter went aboard and dragged the net to the shore. There were 153 large fish, and yet the net hadn't torn.

12 "Now come and have some breakfast!" Jesus said. And no one dared ask him if he really was the Lord because they were sure of it. 13 Then Jesus served them the bread and the fish. 14 This was the third time Jesus had appeared to his disciples since he had been raised from the dead.

21:14
John 20:19, 26

20:31 Some manuscripts read *may continue to believe.*   **21:1** Greek *Sea of Tiberias,* another name for the Sea of Galilee.   **21:2** Greek *the one who was called Didymus.*   **21:8** Greek *200 cubits* [90 meters].

20:27 Jesus' resurrected body was unique. It was not the same kind of flesh and blood Lazarus had when he came back to life. Jesus' body was no longer subject to the same laws of nature as before his death. He could appear in a locked room; yet he was not a ghost or apparition because he could be touched and could eat. Jesus' resurrection was *literal* and *physical*—he was not a disembodied spirit.

20:29 Some people think they would believe in Jesus if they could see a definite sign or miracle. But Jesus says we are blessed if we can believe without seeing. We have all the proof we need in the words of the Bible and the testimony of believers. A physical appearance would not make Jesus any more real to us than he is now.

20:30, 31 To understand the life and mission of Jesus more fully, all we need to do is study the Gospels. John tells us that his Gospel records only a few of the many events in Jesus' life on earth. But the Good News includes everything we need to know to believe that Jesus is the Messiah, the Son of God, through whom we receive eternal life.

21:1ff This chapter tells how Jesus commissioned Peter. Perhaps Peter needed special encouragement after his denial—he may have felt completely worthless. Verses 1-14 set the scene for Jesus' conversation with Peter.

21:7 Only John ("the disciple whom Jesus loved") recognized Jesus in the dim morning light, undoubtedly because Jesus had performed a similar miracle earlier (Luke 5:1-11).

Jesus Challenges Peter (**247**)

21:15
Matt 26:33

[15]After breakfast Jesus said to Simon Peter, "Simon son of John, do you love me more than these?"

"Yes, Lord," Peter replied, "you know I love you."

"Then feed my lambs," Jesus told him.

21:16
Acts 20:28
Heb 13:20-21
1 Pet 5:2-3

[16]Jesus repeated the question: "Simon son of John, do you love me?"

"Yes, Lord," Peter said, "you know I love you."

"Then take care of my sheep," Jesus said.

21:17
John 13:38; 16:30

[17]Once more he asked him, "Simon son of John, do you love me?"

Peter was grieved that Jesus asked the question a third time. He said, "Lord, you know everything. You know I love you."

Jesus said, "Then feed my sheep. [18]The truth is, when you were young, you were able to do as you liked and go wherever you wanted to. But when you are old, you will stretch out your hands, and others will direct you and take you where you don't want to go."

21:19
John 13:36
2 Pet 1:14

[19]Jesus said this to let him know what kind of death he would die to glorify God. Then Jesus told him, "Follow me."

21:20
John 13:23, 25

[20]Peter turned around and saw the disciple Jesus loved following them—the one who had leaned over to Jesus during supper and asked, "Lord, who among us will betray you?" [21]Peter asked Jesus, "What about him, Lord?"

JESUS' APPEARANCES AFTER HIS RESURRECTION		
Mary Magdalene	. . . .	Mark 16:9–11; John 20:11–18
The other women at the tomb	. . . .	Matthew 28:8–10
Peter in Jerusalem	. . . .	Luke 24:34; 1 Corinthians 15:5
The two travelers on the road	. . . .	Mark 16:12, 13
Ten disciples behind closed doors	. . . .	Mark 16:14; Luke 24:36–43; John 20:19–25
All the disciples, with Thomas (excluding Judas Iscariot)	. . . .	John 20:26–31; 1 Corinthians 15:5
Seven disciples while fishing	. . . .	John 21:1–14
Eleven disciples on the mountain	. . . .	Matthew 28:16–20
A crowd of 500	. . . .	1 Corinthians 15:6
Jesus' brother James	. . . .	1 Corinthians 15:7
Those who watched Jesus ascend into heaven	. . . . .	Luke 24:44–49; Acts 1:3–8

The truth of Christianity rests heavily on the Resurrection. If Jesus rose from the grave, who saw him? How trustworthy were the witnesses? Those who claimed to have seen the risen Jesus went on to turn the world upside down. Most of them also died for being followers of Christ. People rarely die for halfhearted belief. These are the people who saw Jesus risen from the grave.

21:15-17 In this beach scene, Jesus led Peter through an experience that would remove the cloud of his denial. Peter had denied Jesus three times. Three times Jesus asked Peter if he loved him. When Peter answered yes, Jesus told him to feed his sheep. It is one thing to say you love Jesus, but the real test is willingness to serve him. Peter had repented, and here Jesus was asking him to commit his life. Peter's life changed when he finally realized who Jesus was. His occupation changed from fisherman to evangelist; his identity changed from impetuous to "rock"; and his relationship to Jesus changed—he was forgiven, and he finally understood the significance of Jesus' words about his death and resurrection.

21:15-17 Jesus asked Peter three times if he loved him. The first time Jesus said, "Do you love (Greek *agape*: volitional, self-sacrificial love) me more than these?" The second time, Jesus focused on Peter alone and still used the word translated into Greek, *agape*. The third time, Jesus used the word translated into Greek, *phileo* (signifying affection, affinity, or brotherly love) and asked, in effect, "Are you even my friend?" Each time Peter responded with the word translated into Greek as *phileo*. Jesus doesn't settle for quick, superficial answers. He has a way of getting to the heart of the matter. Peter had to face his true feelings and motives when Jesus confronted him. How would you respond if Jesus asked you, "Do you love me?" Do you really love Jesus? Are you even his friend?

21:18, 19 This was a prediction of Peter's death by crucifixion. Tradition indicates that Peter was crucified for his faith—upside down because he did not feel worthy of dying as his Lord did. Despite what Peter's future held, Jesus told him to follow him. We may be uncertain and fearful about our future. But if we know God is in control, we can confidently follow Christ.

21:21, 22 Peter asked Jesus how John would die. Jesus replied that Peter should not concern himself with that. We tend to compare our lives to others, whether to rationalize our own level of devotion to Christ or to question God's justice. Jesus responds to us as he did to Peter: "What is that to you? You follow me."

22Jesus replied, "If I want him to remain alive until I return, what is that to you? You follow me." 23So the rumor spread among the community of believers* that that disciple wouldn't die. But that isn't what Jesus said at all. He only said, "If I want him to remain alive until I return, what is that to you?"

24This is that disciple who saw these events and recorded them here. And we all know that his account of these things is accurate.

25And I suppose that if all the other things Jesus did were written down, the whole world could not contain the books.

21:22
Matt 16:27

21:24
John 15:27; 19:35
1 Jn 1:1-3
3 Jn 1:12

21:25
John 20:30

21:23 Greek *the brothers.*

21:23 Early church history reports that after John spent several years as an exile on the island of Patmos, he returned to Ephesus where he died as an old man, near the end of the first century.

21:25   John's stated purpose for writing his Gospel was to show that Jesus was the Son of God (20:31). He clearly and systematically presented the evidence for Jesus' claims. When evidence is presented in the courtroom, those who hear it must make a choice. Those who read the Gospel of John must also make a choice—is Jesus the Son of God, or isn't he? You are the jury. The evidence has been clearly presented. You must decide. Read John's Gospel and believe!

THE COMPLETE *Life Application Study Bible* in the New Living Translation text will be available in local bookstores or through Bibles at Cost in October 1996.

The *Life Application Bible* is also available in the Living Bible text, the New International Version, the King James Version, the New King James Version, and the New Revised Standard Version in a large selection of binding styles. These editions are presently available in local bookstores or through Bibles at Cost (see last two pages).

The *Life Application Bible for Students* is available in the Living Bible text and the New King James Version. The *Kids Application Bible* is available in the Living Bible text.

The *New Believer's Bible* will be available in local bookstores or through Bibles at Cost in November 1996.

Bibles at Cost

To order, call 1-800-778-8865

For Free Shipping Buy 6 Bibles
Pastor, See Next Page for Low-Cost-Start Program
SAVE 40% or more on the best-selling Life Application Bible

Life Application Bible   *List—Our Price*

1. Bonded Leather (NLT, TLB, KJV, NKJV) . . . . $~~60~~ $36.95
2. Large Print Hardcover (only NIV) . . . . $~~47~~ $28.95
3. Deluxe Padded Red or Blue Hardcover (NIV, TLB) . . . . $~~43~~ $24.95
4. Standard Hardcover (NLT, TLB, NIV, KJV, NKJV) . . . . $~~40~~ $23.95

BEST BUY: Hardcover NIV (tan) . . . . **$~~40~~ $22.95**

5. Life Recovery Bible (12-Step/Recovery notes), Hardcover . . $~~25~~ $14.95
6. LAB for Students (ages 11-15), Hardcover (TLB, NKJV) . . . . $~~25~~ $14.95
7. Kid's Application Bible (ages 8-10), Hardcover . . . . $~~20~~ $12.95
8. Eager Reader Bible or God is Great Story Bible (ages 2-8) . $~~16~~ $ 9.95
9. Children's Living Bible, or Family Picture Bible . . . . $~~14~~ $ 6.95
10. 100 Other Bibles, Books, Commentaries, Evangelism Tools, Videos, and Life Application Software . . . . 40% Savings
11. Life Application Study Bible, Gospel of John (62 pages), 400 footnotes, upfront salvation page, and Bible study, only 69¢.

NLT = New Living Translation NIV = New International Version TLB = The Living Bible
KJV = King James Version NKJV = New King James Version

Add $4.00 per order shipping (via UPS, 7 Days or less)
Buy 6 or more Bibles for Free Shipping

TO ORDER: Call toll free 1-800-778-8865 and have your Visa or
Mastercard ready or send check to
Bibles at Cost, 22 Blake Ave., Corralitos, CA 95076

The Life Application Study Bible
Applying God's Word to Today's World

PASTORS: See Low-Cost-Start on next page
Let us help you make these Bibles available at cost at your church.
IT TAKES NO MONEY TO START!

Spread the News—Tell Your Friends
about the Tremendous Savings Available

Bibles at Cost

Your resource for the best-selling family of Life Application Bibles at 30–40% savings for individuals who want one Bible and for churches that need one or more cases of Bibles.

Our Goal

Our goal is to help strengthen the church by providing the family of Life Application Bibles for adults, teens, and kids at a price nearly everyone can afford. We encourage and help churches to make these Bibles available at their tape counter or book table (see Low-Cost-Start below). The low price on these best-selling Bibles has brought a response that is consistently amazing. Sell-outs in one or two weeks are common!

LCS (Low-Cost-Start) Program

Pastors: Whenever a church makes these Bibles available at low cost, the response will be truly amazing. The LCS (Low-Cost-Start) Program means that we help the church by advancing, on consignment, one or more cases of Bibles for resale in the church. The church pays for the Bibles only after they are sold.* If the church chooses to pay for the Bibles at the time they place the order with us, then an additional 5% is deducted from the already discounted price. This is a real opportunity to make these wonderful Bibles available—at near ¢ cost and without risk. Many churches are now participating in our LCS Program, and their testimony is one of continued satisfaction. Join us—you will be glad you did. A maximum of $600 of inventory is advanced on consignment with a one-third ($200) deposit.

Call us for savings on:

- New Living Translation—Deluxe Text Edition, New Believer's New Testament, Life Application Study Bible, and New Believer's Bible
- Bible Study Tools—Commentaries, Dictionaries, etc.
- Children's Ministry and VBS Specials—Save up to 60%
- Evangelism Specials, New Testaments, or more copies of this special Gospel of John at 69¢ each
- This Gospel of John contains over 400 application notes; it's a great evangelism tool.

To order, call 1-800-778-8865